THE P-A-I-D EDUCATOR

Copyright © 2020 by Dr. Bisa Batten Lewis

All rights reserved. No part of this book may be reproduced in any written, electronic, recording, or photocopying without written permission of the publisher or author. The exception would be in the case of brief quotations embodied on the pages where the publisher or author specifically grants permission.

Books may be purchased in quantity and/or special sales by contacting the publisher.

Mynd Matters Publishing
715 Peachtree Street NE
Suites 100 & 200
Atlanta, GA 30308
www.myndmatterspublishing.com

978-1-948145-65-7 (pbk)
978-1-948145-68-8 (hdcvr)
978-1-948145-66-44 (ebook)

Library of Congress Control Number: 2019919814

FIRST EDITION

Printed in the United States of America

THE P-A-I-D EDUCATOR

10 PROFESSIONAL WAYS TO SUPPLEMENT YOUR TEACHING SALARY

Bisa Batten Lewis, EdD

To Mrs. Burson, Mrs. Suttles, Dr. Campbell and every educator who recognized my flicker.

CONTENTS

INTRODUCTION 9

PART I: Getting P-A-I-D for Reading 17

    Chapter One: EDITING 19

    Chapter Two: PROOFREADING 29

    Chapter Three: RESEARCHING 35

Part II: Getting P-A-I-D for Writing 45

    Chapter Four: GRANTS 47

    Chapter Five: WEB CONTENT 63

    Chapter Six: ARTICLES 77

Part III: Getting P-A-I-D for Speaking 89

    Chapter Seven: PRESENTING 91

    Chapter Eight: CONSULTING 105

Part IV: Getting P-A-I-D for Selling 117

    Chapter Nine: PRODUCTS 119

    Chapter Ten: PERFORMANCES 135

CONCLUSION 143

SPECIAL ACKNOWLEDGMENTS 163

ABOUT THE AUTHOR.................................. 165

INTRODUCTION

Don't limit yourself!
Teaching is awesome, but there is so much more!

Bravo! Take a moment to pat yourself on the back. Celebrate yourself for purchasing this book. You've taken a meaningful first step by investing in yourself and your desire to make a change. Whether you are an educator or administrator in a preschool, grade school, college, or community program, you're about to learn how to get P-A-I-D—on your own terms. And, don't feel guilty. You're not alone by a longshot!

The National Center for Education Statistics (NCES) periodically publishes new analyses from the National Teacher and Principal Survey (NTPS) dataset and has reported "nearly one in five public school teachers have second jobs during the school year," and half of those jobs are outside the education profession. They've also reported "55% of teachers say they are not satisfied with their teaching salaries."

Not only are teachers displeased about their significantly low salaries compared to other similarly skilled professions, there are many issues driving them away from the profession, including student discipline concerns, developmentally inappropriate expectations of children, unrealistic and overwhelming expectations of teachers, physical conditions of buildings and classrooms, emotional stress, lack of basic classroom supplies, large class sizes, lack of respect from students and their parents, high-stakes standardized testing, lack of administrative support and the list goes on, to the point where during the 2018-2019 school year, which was labeled "tumultuous," hundreds of thousands of educators participated in walkouts and pay disputes across the country and record numbers called it quits. Do any of these reports surprise you? Thought not. So, enough of what we already know. Let's move on to the solutions.

This book will teach you how to use your education, work experience, and talents to supplement your current income if you'd like to continue working full-time in a school, educational program, or institution. You will also learn how to start and build your own business to a level that will enable you to totally replace your income if you're considering resigning from your full-time position. The choice is yours. I just want you to know you can, and it's possible. My career is the perfect example!

In the early 1990's, while studying early childhood education as an undergrad at Albany State University, I was fortunate to enroll in Mrs. Burson's education literacy course. As she discussed different topics related to the importance of engaging children in daily literacy experiences, along with the varying strategy recommendations based on each child's reading level, she'd sometimes digress to share anecdotes from her consulting work and former job as an editor at a well-known and highly respected education publishing company, where she still worked part time as a consultant. I fell in love with the word "consultant." I sat in the front row of the class, just waiting for Mrs. Burson to interpose another professional experience. Although my peers seemed agitated by her anecdotes and digressions about her work outside of the classroom, I was all ears and would even take notes.

Eventually, Mrs. Burson noticed how intrigued I was. Shortly after, she started taking me on consulting gigs as her workshop assistant. We traveled from Georgia to Florida conducting workshops, primarily to support parents of children diagnosed with Attention Deficit Disorder (ADD) and Attention Deficit with Hyperactivity Disorder (ADHD). I'd watch in amazement as parents shared their stories, some even crying, about the high doses of medication required to keep their children safe from their own spontaneous actions, aggression, and/or hyperactivity. Then, Mrs. Burson would sweep in to save the day, drying their tears by offering professional recommendations from both perspectives of an educator and a mother who could empathetically relate, having a child with learning disabilities herself. Mrs. Burson showed me a new realm of the education profession, and I was eager to learn more—not just for the money, but to be the professional who revives the light in people's eyes and relieves the pressure from their heads and chests. You see, I discovered that helping others helps me.

Fast-forward to present day. While earning four degrees, including a B.S. degree, two M.Ed. degrees, and a Doctor of Education degree, I've founded two companies—an education consulting firm and a curriculum company. You know those books and materials schools purchase for teachers to implement in the classroom with children? Yep, I wrote my own learning system, and it continues to pay off. How about all those professional development opportunities you're *voluntold* to take advantage of at work. Yep, I get paid to do those too. I've actually expanded the company to the level where I am able to employ colleagues to present workshops and provide consulting services. I also get paid to consult with toy companies on mommy-baby products, faith-based projects, celebrity youth programs, TV, film, and much more! The progression of technology and social media has made the world smaller, leading to an increase in opportunities around the country and abroad. Finally, I'm getting paid what I'm worth! We can't wait for HR to give us the pay raises we want and need. We must go get them for ourselves.

Over the years, I've shared business and part-time employment ideas with other colleagues, but many of them couldn't see outside of the system. It was as if they were mentally and emotionally imprisoned, thinking they HAD to have a job to live well. Although they'd encouraged their students, on a daily basis, to reach for the stars, they weren't reaching themselves. Instead, they were settling, waiting years or even decades to reach retirement age, before they could live their desired lives. Tomorrow isn't promised to us, so forget retiring at fifty-nine and a half or sixty-five. Give me my fortune while I'm full of energy and young enough to enjoy it! Are you with me? I want ALL my fellow education colleagues to assess their abilities and determine how to truly use what they've experienced and learned to get the riches they desire. We work so hard to encourage and pour into others. Well, it's hightime we pour into ourselves!

The acronym P-A-I-D conceptualizes the groundwork you will be coached to complete throughout this book. **P-A-I-D** stands for **P**rospects-**A**llies-**I**nformation-**D**ollars.

Prospects: Possible goods, services, events, occupations and clients

Allies: Human resources—individuals and groups with capacities to support

Information: Facts and evidence obtained through observation, investigation or experience

Dollars: Various amounts of money you can make for goods and services

As you read and progress through the "self-work" necessary to supplement or replace your current income, you will need to keep the meaning of each element of the acronym in mind. But, don't worry about remembering each element. I will remind you when it's necessary to reflect. If you're an educator, think of the P-A-I-D Self-Work in each chapter as your personal lesson plan for your career. If you're an administrator, think of the P-A-I-D Self-Work as your operational plan for personal success. Conceptualize this work as you do the regular school reports and data you receive about your class, school, or program's success—as if the lack of this work could result in your school or program losing accreditation, funding, or being placed on a low-performance or school closure list. How can you have a performance plan for your job, but not for yourself? Come on! What they tell us about developing lesson plans to teach our classes and annual plans to assess our professional development and progress each school year is true, "If you fail to plan, you plan to fail." Educators must remember to apply standards of planning at both work *and* home.

Throughout these pages, I won't just share with you all the ways I get paid and how other educators I've interviewed get paid outside of the classroom, but the different ways you can use your own knowledge and skills to get paid. Whether you decide to keep your full-time job or quit it, you CAN treat yourself to a bigger budget if you plan accordingly. Go ahead and think about all the ways you'd like to spend and save your new fortune. Is it more travel? An RV? A new hobby? More outings with your family or your boo? Early retirement? Whatever you want to do, you CAN do! The answers are just a few pages away. Come on and get P-A-I-D! There's no time like the present.

PART I:
Getting P-A-I-D for Reading

1.
EDITING

Make change making changes.

Back in the early 1990's, when I was an undergraduate student in college, I had the pleasure of becoming one of Mrs. Burson's mentees, along with my *brother from another mother*, Johnny—my father's son who I learned about later in life. Neither of us realized we were both mentees of Mrs. Burson, until one day she nearly screamed when she found out we were siblings. Johnny was the quarterback on our college football team and eventually became a respected minister on campus and in the community, while working as a full-time high school football coach. Mrs. Burson treated us both like her own children. She would have us over to her beautiful home in the most prominent neighborhood in the city. We knew all her family members by name, and they knew us just the same. I would even tutor her youngest son in their beautiful open dining/living room. Our relationship blossomed and left a lasting impression on both Johnny and me, especially since Mrs. Burson was one of very few white faculty members in the College of Education at our HBCU. At that time, I had only seen homes like theirs on soap operas and wondered how a college instructor and high school football coach could live so well. Mrs. Burson always dressed professionally and in garments made of expensive-looking fabrics. Silk and suede appeared to be her favorites. She always looked neat and well put together. When she would arrive home from work, she'd go in the kitchen to cook while checking her children's homework and asking about their day, just like families I'd only seen on television. Because my mom worked at a factory on 'swing shifts' for most of my childhood, my dad was a musician on the road playing bass guitar for celebrities, and my stepfather operated his own landscaping business working until dusk each day, watching the Bursons as a guest in their home—and the Huxtables on *The Cosby Show*—was how I formed the concept of the kind of life I wanted to live—a PAID life filled with love from a close-knit family. One thing I knew for sure was I had to learn more about how Mrs. Burson made money outside of the classroom. I was happy she didn't mind sharing with me and showing me the ropes.

Aside from the workshops she conducted, she often spoke of editing for a publishing company, which published many of the textbooks I'd seen in my education courses.

Thirteen years later, I moved from Albany, Georgia to the south side of Atlanta. Little did I know, Mrs. Burson had moved as well, and only lived three exits away. My brother Johnny and his family also lived in the Atlanta area about an hour away. Mrs. Burson and I connected on Facebook and couldn't wait to meet up. We met for lunch at my favorite Mediterranean restaurant in Peachtree City, The BeiRut, which she had yet to try. We shared an appetizer platter of falafel, hummus, naan, and other healthy faves we'd chosen together. Mrs. Burson looked as healthy and affluent as ever. She was now a grandmother and remarried. Encouragingly, she was still working part-time as an editor and was no longer working as an educator. Although I had become very successful in my own career, which I thanked her for repeatedly, I was still intrigued and wondered what being an editor involved.

After conducting my own research, I learned that editing involves making changes and suggestions to improve the overall quality of one's writing, particularly in relation to language use and expression. After editing, the writer's language should be sharp and consistent with clear expression and enhanced overall readability. Editing occurs prior to proofreading.

The Benefits of Editing
- Overall quality of writing improved
- Language-use enhanced
- Expression clearer
- Errors and inconsistencies removed
- Your writing will have maximum impact

www.experteditor.com

There are different types of editors and based on the resource you consult, the list may vary. I reached out to Mrs. Burson to interview her for this book and find out her specific role as an editor for the major educational textbook company she worked with for decades. She shared her role was to "offer strategies and techniques that work best with children," ensuring the methods described in the textbooks were based on current practices within the education profession that could be adapted based on children's individual needs and goals. She profoundly added the different strategies written in the textbooks should take the readers, who were primarily educators or prospective educators, "from *knowledge* to *understanding* to *application*." As you explore opportunities for editing, here are some roles to consider.

- **Copy Editors** review and correct written material to improve accuracy, readability, and appropriateness based on purpose, as well as ensure it is free of error, omission, inconsistency, and repetition.

- **Content Editors** evaluate overall formatting, style, and content of a document to optimize visual design and comprehensibility.

- **Commissioning Editors** advise the publishing house on which books to publish.

- **Editors-in-Chief** are the journalistic leaders for publications and have final responsibility for operations and policies.

- **Literary Editors** deal with aspects concerning literature, books, and reviews by providing proofreading, copy-editing, and literary criticism.

- **Managing Editors** are senior members of a publication's management team and oversee all aspects of the publication.

- **Contributing Editors** are often upscale freelancers, consultants or experts with proven abilities and readership attraction.

- **Fashion Editors** supervise the process of creating, developing and presenting content for the fashion department of a magazine, website, newspaper or television program.

- **Political Editors** cover politics and related matters for newspaper, radio or television.

- **Assignment Editors** select, develop and plan reporting assignments for news events or feature stories at newspaper, radio or television stations, to be covered by reporters.

- **Photo Editors** collect, review, and choose

photographs and/or photo illustrations for publication based on pre-determined guidelines.

- **City Editors** track news and are responsible for the daily changes of a particular issue of a newspaper scheduled to be released the following day.

As you consider *Ps (prospects)* for editing, think about the publications you read or listen to most frequently. That's a great place to start. Go online to their webpages and find out if there are any current opportunities that interest you. Peruse their current list of staff members to see if you recognize any names who might become your *As (allies)*. The advancement of technology continues to increase and improve the services available online to recruit and hire editors. No face-to-face or traditional exchange is even necessary any longer. Based on the chosen software application, potential editors and clients can correspond within the tool of choice and never exchange contact information. Reedsy, Upwork, Freelancer, and Fiverr are just a few of the modernized service tools for editors seeking opportunities. If you are interested in editing, you should check out those websites and explore client posts requesting editors. I have fellow author friends who have used these websites and I've even used them myself to contract editors. Trust me, they make good money! There are many posts and requests just waiting for your click. Heck, go ahead and setup an account right now.

Nowadays, many publications are *only* available online, which significantly reduces the costs associated with printing and distribution. Any modern newspaper, magazine or journal worth its salt has an online edition, whether they continue to print or not. Think about your favorite professional publications, and even those you enjoy reading as a hobby. Someone had to edit each article and component, long before it reached libraries, bookstores, or your mailbox. Several editors were involved in editing this book. I wonder how many are/were educators getting paid to edit this book as a side gig or now a full-time career. I was told there was at least one and this is just one book! Think about the total number of books a publishing company releases each year—heck, each month. This could have been your opportunity to get P-A-I-D! Your goals are just waiting on you to make the decision to get started.

Television and radio broadcasting are even available online and in various formats. Consider your current television and radio preferences. Whether you enjoy listening to radio via analog, digital, internet, or Sirius XM, or watching television via analog, cable, satellite, digital, or internet, remember they all need editors! The next time you watch a television show or movie, take time to read the credits at the end. You'll be amazed at all the roles necessary to broadcast a program.

Today's editors can work from the comfort of their homes and accept contracts from as many clients as their eyes, fingers and bandwidth can handle. If you currently or previously taught language arts or any other subject requiring extensively reading and correcting students' writing, you might strongly consider supplementing, and later replacing, your income by working as an editor. You don't have to start big or with an impressive website; just start with one client and add on from there. It's time for you to do the self-work to get P-A-I-D for editing. Just answer the listed questions and act on your responses.

SELF-WORK:
Getting P-A-I-D for Editing

Prospects
What goods, services, events, occupations and clients need editing?

Allies
Which individuals and groups have capacities to support my editing goals?

Information
What do I already know about editing?

What do I want and need to learn about editing?

What resources (books, articles, websites, specialists/experts, etc.) can support my efforts to improve my editing knowledge and skills?

Dollars
How much money can I make editing?

What next step will I make to begin getting P-A-I-D for editing?

2.
PROOFREADING

One man's error is another man's treasure!

Proofreading is the process of looking for and correcting surface errors in writing, such as grammatical, typographical, spelling, punctuation and other language mistakes (experteditor.com). Proofreading is not as involved or complicated as editing, nevertheless the process is necessary to publish any type of writing.

Mrs. Suttles, my seventh grade English teacher was the first to make a big deal of my writing. She regularly complimented my assignment submissions, whether they were poems, essays, narratives, or just a paragraph. As a result, from middle school throughout high school, I was a confident writer and earned high scores on assignments in my English/Language Arts classes. Any time a teacher gave an assignment to write about a topic, I knew I'd do well. Then, I entered college, where my English 101 instructor Ms. Penn burst my bubble. She had the audacity to require me to spend ten hours per week in the writing lab. She said my writing needed to be "more sophisticated," so I had to learn the appropriate use of conjunctions. Just when I thought I knew the rules, they changed, and seem to continue to do so.

The Benefits of Proofreading
- Spelling, grammar, and typing mistakes eliminated
- Consistent language and formatting
- Perfection of already good writing
- Ensures a publication-ready document
- Cheaper than editing

www.experteditor.com

After completing my Bachelor of Science Degree in Early Childhood Education, I was hired as a first-grade teacher at a public elementary school. Guess who walked in my classroom for Open House with her niece of whom she now had guardianship—Ms. Penn. I'd been secretly carrying a slight grudge against her for sending me to the writing lab, however, by this time, I realized she was right and appreciated how much I learned during all those hours of listening to recordings about appropriate grammar use and sentence structure, writing drafts, and receiving feedback from the writing lab instructors and student workers. Ms. Penn became one of my biggest supporters in my career and continues to cheer me on. I wonder if she gets P-A-I-D to proofread, outside of her position at the university. I will have to ask her the next time she attends one of my speaking engagements.

As you seek out proofreading opportunities, you may find the average person makes little distinction between editing and may use "editor" when an actual proofreader is needed. Be sure to read the entire post, request, or job announcement, before submitting a reply. You might also ask some clarifying questions about the opportunity to ensure you know exactly what the client wants. Don't be surprised if the client doesn't know the difference him/herself. Think about it, that's why a professional who *does* know the difference between a proofreader and editor needs to be hired. I like working with clients who know what they *don't* know and how to stay in their lanes. I love being free to be creative. The process of writing *The P-A-I-D Educator* has been quite the eye-opener, as I've gone through the multiple editing and proofreading processes. Each time I've received a draft copy, I continue to add on more information and think about what the reader might want to learn from each chapter. The best thing about the experience is there are NEVER any errors when I view it. This publisher has great editors AND proofreaders on staff who are carefully reading each word from cover to cover.

Any educator who teaches English/Language Arts should strongly consider becoming a proofreader as a side hustle and possibly expand to full-time. You can work from home and get PAID to point out mistakes. Think about the different documents and publications you can support—online and in print. According to the Bureau of Labor Statistics (BLS), the average pay for a full-time proofreader is $20.17 per hour and $41,950 per year.[1] Considering the many industries in need of proofreaders—publishers, newspapers, television, magazines, journals, blogs, legal services, motion picture/video, business support, religious

---

[1] https://www.bls.gov/oes/current/oes439081.htm

organizations and more, your earnings could exceed the average, if you are resourceful.

If you want to start a career freelancing as a proofreader, you will need to do the self-work necessary to gain knowledge about the craft and opportunities that enable you to supplement or replace your income. Start with freelancing websites, such as Upwork, Freelancer, Reedsy, Fiverr, Fancy Hands, and Work-At-Home Moms (WAHM). Publishers, such as Amazon KDP, and bloggers are always in need of editors and proofreaders, so consider those websites as well. You can even find some proofreading positions on job boards, such as Indeed, Glassdoor, and ProBlogger.

SELF-WORK:
Getting P-A-I-D for Proofreading

Prospects
What goods, services, events, occupations and clients need proofreading?

Allies
Which individuals and groups have capacities to support my proofreading goals?

Information
What do I already know about proofreading?

What do I want and need to learn about proofreading?

What resources (books, articles, sites, specialists/experts, etc.) can support my efforts to improve my proofreading knowledge and skills?

Dollars
How much money can I make for proofreading?

What next step will I make to begin getting P-A-I-D for proofreading?

3.
RESEARCHING

Reading is supplemental.

How did you feel when you were charged with conducting research in high school and college? How good were your research skills compared to your classmates? Did your research skills improve over time? Be honest. Was Google even a thing when you were in college? Well, whether you learned to conduct research in a brick and mortar library or on the World Wide Web, you can get PAID to conduct research for others. Think about it. The average person hates conducting research! It's time to make their pain your gain!

Whether I was teaching first graders, high schoolers

or college students, I often found it necessary to conduct research to prepare for classes. As a first-grade teacher in the mid-1990s, I recall creating a lesson around bats, primarily to teach the beginning sound "B." As my students showed increasing interest and curiosity around bats, I ended up developing an entire thematic unit around bats. Having little knowledge about bats myself, at the time, I found myself conducting seemingly endless research to learn more about the different types of bats, their habitats, diets, geographical locations, size of their wings and thumbs, etc. The topics related to bats went on and on, to the point where I was able to teach skills from each developmental domain and cover learning standards from every academic subject. If only Teachers Pay Teachers was available back then. I would have racked up on developing thematic units for educators and reached billionaire status by now. I eventually parlayed my ability to research and write lesson plans for educators into a regular hefty paycheck, but I'll save that story for the chapter on Products.

One research contract I had didn't involve much pay, but provided me a variety of equipment and materials to utilize in other areas of my work in the community. I was practically classified as a research consultant who evaluated learning materials to see if they were appropriate for preschool classrooms. The perk was being able to keep all of the items shipped to my house. On any given day, I might have a toddler trampoline in one corner and a stack of children's science experiment sets, books, and music CDs in another. My house sometimes looked like a family childcare program. After receiving the materials, I had to complete the prescribed form confirming whether the materials were appropriate for the specified age group. This was a fun contract! Interestingly, I didn't even seek it out. I was simply engaging in a friendly conversation with a vendor at a conference. I had no idea she was a 'heavy-hitter' in the company and would soon be promoted to Vice President. After that event, she always remembered me and how easily we were able to hold candid conversations and bounce ideas off of one another. I mention this particular contract to help you to understand that everything you do can't be about money. I've offered a myriad of services, and even products, for free, before I was able to branch out to the point where I was paid and sought after.

I interviewed a colleague who is a former toddler and preschool teacher to ask how she's been able to work independently, after starting her own company.

Although she eventually became a consultant/trainer, her responses are actually grounded in research. Regina Folks-Amerson was born in California and raised in Mississippi. As an adult, her career sprouted in Pittsburgh, Pennsylvania where she worked on grant projects, primarily for nonprofit organizations, such as the YWCA, after teaching in the classroom and advancing to administration. You see, conducting research is necessary to write any grant proposal and to operate any type of program. When I asked Regina about her success and what advice she'd give educators who want to supplement their income and even start their own businesses, she shared the importance of connecting with programs and resources, along with being able to articulate information. To move from the classroom to administration and eventually to being her own boss, Regina stresses the importance of keeping one's knowledge current, which further enhances a professional's ability to effectively communicate.

"You have to be better than everyone else," she said, "Be the expert." She further advised, "You have to lose your pride."

As early educators, even if you've advanced to administration, you may find yourself changing an infant's diaper, sweeping the floor, or stepping up to complete some task no one else wants to do. That's what a good leader does. What are you gonna do? Keep walking over that pile of trash until someone else cleans it up? Reaching one's full potential requires us to do the "dirty work" on the way up. In Regina's words, "You have to learn, earn, and then return." Meaning, once you've done the research and learned how to do something and make money doing it, you must give back. Like Regina, I learned everything I know along the way, some through research and others through trial and error. But one thing I know for sure, if I didn't know how to research using trusted publications, I definitely would not be where I am today.

When I was teaching at Albany State University, I had an amazing student intern, who was also a presidential scholar. Christina was her name. After consulting with colleagues who were already authors, especially one of our deans, Dr. Barbara Brown, I knew I wanted to write books. Luckily, I had Christina, one of the university's top student scholars, to conduct the research for me and make folders for each chapter of the behavior/classroom management textbook, which I NEVER wrote. I had a publisher waiting and everything! Although I did end up writing chapters in several textbooks used in classes at the college level, I always wondered why I never followed through on that particular book. Reflecting on the experience, I honestly believe it was because I wasn't connected to it. I needed to do the part Christina was doing and research the information myself.

One of my most recent contracts involved me conducting research and writing a national publication to support educators. The client is a nonprofit organization with partners around the country and abroad. When I accepted the contract, the Scope of Work appeared manageable, so I signed the contract without hesitation, especially since I'd built such a great relationship with senor staff there. My goal was to make them proud and not let them down, while producing for them a product of which we could all be proud. The research I had to conduct consumed my life for five months. However, I gained even more self-respect for my own skills. There were moments when I became insecure and wondered what I'd gotten myself into. Then, I'd give myself a pep talk, which I learned from Jen Sincero's books *You Are a Badass* and *You Are a Badass at Making Money*. In her books, Jen tells us, "Raise your frequency" to make 'ish' happen. So, that's exactly what I did. Even though I realized similar publications involved multiple researchers on the project, instead of just one—little ol' me, I got out of my own head and put myself on a schedule to get the job done. Whether I needed to maximize internet searches or reach out to professionals I'd met who regularly engaged in the processes we were researching, I was adamant about delivering beneficial research in a format educators could use to implement the program.

Years ago, I discovered my preferred work time is in the middle of the night—all night when it's crunch time. I decided to forgive myself, knowing I didn't have to wake up at 4:40 AM anymore to teach in the local school system. I could stay up late to research and sleep until the following afternoon if I wanted. This was not a common practice, but it served me well at times, since I could better concentrate when the house was quiet and everyone was in bed.

Researchers are useful to a variety of industries, including news, health, medicine, sports, education, culinary, politics, technology and so on. As an educator, you must conduct research to properly prepare to teach lessons related to your subject area. Have you ever wondered who might benefit from some of the research you identify and implement in your classes? Whether you teach math, science, social studies, language arts, or an elective, your content is needed to achieve someone's daily career objectives and challenges. Take a moment to write down all the topics you teach each school year, or simply pull out your course content schedule and highlight our faves. Then, go online to FlexJobs.com to locate at least one post requiring the information you teach students every day.

Now, it's time to complete the self-work required for you to get P-A-I-D to conduct research.

SELF-WORK:
Getting P-A-I-D for Researching

Prospects
What goods, services, events, occupations and clients need researchers?

Allies
Which individuals and groups have capacity to support my research goals?

Information
What do I already know about conducting research?

What do I want and need to learn about conducting research?

What resources (books, articles, websites, experts, etc.) can support my efforts to improve my research skills?

Dollars
How much money can I make as a researcher?

What next step will I make to begin getting P-A-I-D to conduct research?

Part II:
Getting P-A-I-D for Writing

4.
GRANTS

Be your own pen pal!

Preparing successful grant proposals can aid in the acquisition of funds for quality improvement, program startup, community services, and other desired projects. The primary skill involved in grant writing is simply following directions, which the average person seems to lack in totality. Think about how many forms you've sent home to parents that were returned incomplete. Or, better yet, consider forms you've administered to colleagues that were returned incomplete. If following directions is your strength, then grant writing may be a skill you can develop to get P-A-I-D.

In 1998, while teaching first grade at a public school in Dougherty County in Albany, Georgia, I accepted a summer job working as Math and Science Coordinator in the Albany State University (ASU) National Youth Sports Program (NYSP), which was primarily funded by the United States Department of Agriculture (USDA), the U.S. Department of Health and Human Services, and the National Collegiate Athletic Association (NCAA). I was excited about working for NYSP, because my sister and I participated in the summer program during our youth.

As the NYSP Math and Science Coordinator, I was considered one of the program's administrators. Therefore, I was involved in numerous meetings with the ASU faculty and staff who managed NYSP on the campus. This was the first time I experienced feeling like a true professional in my field. In our meetings, my opinions were valued and often requested. I was given access to information and technology that wasn't yet utilized in our public schools. I really felt like someone important.

I was, eventually, invited by the Department Chair of Health, Physical Education and Recreation, Dr. Wilburn Campbell, to collaborate on writing a grant proposal to increase the number of prospective science, technology, engineering, and mathematics (STEM) teachers. Although I'd never written a grant proposal before, I accepted the opportunity, knowing I wouldn't have to do it alone. We met for several weeks, in collaboration with faculty from the ASU College of Arts and Sciences, to complete the grant proposal. We titled our proposal "The Science Connection Project for Middle and High School Recruitment," which ended up being funded at $50,000 for the 1998-1999 academic year. The budget included a $4,000 stipend for me as the Program Coordinator. This was a dream come true for me as a moderately experienced educator and first-time grant writer.

The first year's program experienced tremendous success and was developed around forty high school and middle school students ranging from ages thirteen to sixteen, five student mentors, five teachers of excellence, and a Science Researcher involved with ASU and the National Aeronautics and Space Administration (NASA). The project was implemented in conjunction with ASU NYSP, ASU Arts and Sciences Faculty, Dougherty County School System middle and high school faculty, the P-16 Council, and the Marine Corps Logistics Base (MCLB), during the summer of 1999. The objectives of the Science Connection Project for Middle and High School

Recruitment were to provide:

- Middle and high school students the opportunity to strengthen knowledge about science, and to improve their level of understanding in the use of scientific processes.

- An opportunity for middle and high school students to learn about careers in science-related fields, especially science educators.

- Increased exposure to technology use and improve written communication and study skills.

- Middle school students exposure to College of Education programs and increase understanding of college accessibility.

- Stimulating mathematical learning experiences through innovative teaching techniques.

- Active participation in a nationally recognized scientific experiment with NASA involving a butterfly project.

- An opportunity to recruit potential science education majors from the Marine Corps Logistics Center military personnel and use the center as a training site.

In 1999, I was hired as a full-time Early Childhood Education Instructor at ASU, after working in the Dougherty County School System for six years—two years as a first-grade paraprofessional and four years as a first-grade teacher. Excitingly, our grant project was funded for another year. Dr. Campbell and I shortened the name to the Science Initiative Project, which we referred to as SIP. You know how much we educators love an acronym! The program featured hands-on scientific experimentation, use of technology, and experimental and traditional methodologies related to teaching mathematical concepts. The culminating experience involved a collaborative research experiment consisting of a Butterfly Project, an expansion of the initial curriculum. Highlights of the program included field trips to Calloway Gardens in Pine Mountain, Georgia and the Coca Cola Space Center in Atlanta.

As all soft money usually does, the funding ended. So, as we grant writers often do, Dr. Campbell and I found another funding source. However, we had to change the name of the program and tweak its objectives to fit the new funding. We decided to call the new program the Albany State University Youth Teacher Academy, which was affectionately referred to as YTA. It became an extension of SIP and was implemented in March 2001 with a grant award of over

$46,000. Twenty-two applicants were selected as Student Interns, who ranged from high school juniors to college seniors, in addition to three paraprofessionals currently working in the Dougherty County School System. Two of the Student Interns were selected to work as Student Mentors in NYSP for four weeks. The Student Mentors assisted the NYSP Math and Science Coordinator (me) in implementing innovative activities for program participants, whose ages ranged from ten to sixteen. Computer Technology classes were provided to NYSP participants by the YTA Student Mentors, who had been engaged in extensive professional development presented by consultants we contracted with to plan the technology component of the curriculum.

The objectives of YTA were to:

- Recruit teachers in the areas of science, math, and other teaching fields.

- Provide students with meaningful experiences in science, mathematics, reading, and extra-curricular activities.

- Expose program participants to model teachers in critical teaching fields.

- Develop a collaborative effort, through several existing programs, to ensure the project is enduring.

- Participate with the University's P-16 Collaborative to continue promoting and fostering a strong and positive relationship with local middle school and high school counselors.

- Provide meaningful post-secondary experiences for college students and teacher assistants who have demonstrated an interest and promise as future teachers.

- Develop and involve students in a structured program involving pedagogy and Foundations of Education.

- Provide ways and means to ensure each participant has positive hands-on experiences in the use of technology.

The 2001 project was developed around five modules:
1. Technology
2. Service Learning
3. Professional Development
4. Teacher Education Admission
5. Leadership

The technology component was implemented through collaboration with an independent technology corporation and the ASU Educational Technology Training Center. The participants were trained to create web pages on which they could post resumes, contact information and electronic portfolios. The program participants were required to attend seminars to satisfy the objectives that corresponded with this module:

- Introduction to Technology
- Constructing Self-Brochures w/ MS Publisher
- Database Design Using MS Access
- Developing an Electronic Portfolio
- Web Page Construction w/ Netscape
- Web Page Construction w/ FrontPage

The Service-Learning module was implemented in two innovative ways:

1. The student interns and mentors constructed learning materials at the Georgia Learning Resources System (GLRS). After one week (ten total hours) of constructing developmentally appropriate learning materials, the students implemented the games and activities with children enrolled at Jackson Heights Child

Development Center—one of ASU's two off-site lab schools. The interns donated the materials to the center.

2. After attending two seminars, "Learning Modalities and Multiple Intelligences" and "Gross and Fine Motor Skill Development," the participants utilized the appropriate developmental equipment to enhance gross and fine motor skills of children enrolled in Jackson Heights Child Development Center. Each YTA student intern and mentor was required to complete a minimum of twenty hours of field experience at the lab school.

Admission to Teacher Education had become a dilemma for many students interested in the teaching profession due to the requirement to pass the Praxis I examination prior to applying for admission. Therefore, YTA offered seminars to prepare students for Praxis I. These seminars were presented by selected faculty in the ASU Department of Mathematics and the Department of Learning Support. The grant funding enabled us to pay our colleagues for their services.

Dr. Campbell eventually became the Interim Dean

of the College of Education. I considered him my number one A-ally! Under his leadership, my grant writing skills continued to progress. I was able to write numerous grant proposals ranging from $4,000 to $326,000, including a large application with a team of colleagues that landed the university a state-of-the-art on-site child development center, which serves as a lab school and still stands today. I had learned from the Vice President of Fiscal Affairs, who I knew well from high school and college, another ally, that faculty could earn up to one-third of our salary during the months of June and July, since we were only paid a ten-month salary. That one tidbit of information fueled me to do just that. I was able to supplement my college faculty income by an additional one-third by writing grant proposals and including myself as a staffer. Yep, I aimed for the max and earned it!

As I continued to write for funding, one issue I wanted to resolve for early educators was the acceptance of course credit from one college level to the next. I collaborated with about three other colleagues at the university to write the HBCU/Head Start Partnership grant, which enabled us to support Head Start teachers in earning their Associate and Baccalaureate degrees. We were able to provide college courses at their job site, purchase laptops and textbooks, as well as provide a stipend to support the Head Start teachers with school supplies and transportation. One of our major feats was securing approval of an articulation agreement between Albany Technical College (ATC) and ASU for students' course credits to transfer from the Associate Degree Program at ATC to the Baccalaureate program at ASU. Prior to that time, early childhood education majors had to start from scratch to secure the next level credential. Leading the charge to secure signatures from presidents of both institutions was an esteemed moment in my career.

After successfully writing grants for a number of years and connecting with various organizations to engage in community service, I was eventually sought after as a grant reviewer. This role involved reading submitted grant proposals to determine which met the funding criteria. Similarly, I have served as a grant evaluator, which involved reviewing programs at the end of the funding period to determine whether they met the deliverables outlined in their proposal. While neither of these roles are usually compensated, serving as a grant reviewer or grant evaluator enables you to sharpen your skills as a grant writer. You're able to learn more about the key components of a grant proposal, the profile of grant proposals that are generally funded, and most importantly, what NOT to do when writing a grant proposal.

There are plenty of resources out there to support your efforts in learning to follow the instructions in grant applications. I highly recommend investing in *The Foundation Center's Guide to Proposal Writing*, in addition to subscribing to the Foundation Directory Online.[2]

The Foundation Center[3] is the world's leading source of information on philanthropy, fundraising, and grant programs. Do yourself a favor and take some time to peruse the plethora of resources on the Foundation Center website. You may find the need to start, or partner with, a nonprofit to qualify for much of the funding. As educators, we often spend our own money to support students, colleagues, or some cause that is near and dear to our hearts. Well, guess what? You don't have to continue spending your own funds. There are plenty of funds out there. All you have to do is find out who is doing the work related to your cause and get connected—by signing up for their email/newsletter distribution list, volunteering, joining

---

[2] fconline.foundationcenter.org/
[3] foundationcenter.org

their board or advisory committee, and/or even inviting them to visit or speak to your class, student club, organization, or program.

Perusing the websites of local institutions of higher education can support your grant goals. Colleges and universities often utilize grant funds to operate. You just need to find out what programs are being funded that relate to your professional goals and talents. View the program's faculty/staff list to find out who you know that might serve as your ally.

Now, it's time for you to complete the self-work required to get P-A-I-D for grants. Start by thinking of a service needed in your community that you would provide if money wasn't a challenge, and don't forget about services you already volunteer.

SELF-WORK:
Getting P-A-I-D for Writing Grants

Prospects

What service(s) have I wanted to provide, but didn't have the funding?

Who do I know that writes grant proposals?

Who do I know that might need a grant writer?

Who do I know that is currently receiving grant funding?

Allies

Which individuals and groups will support my grant writing goals?

Who would be a valuable addition to my grant writing team?

Which individuals and groups will enable me to learn about grant writing by working on their team or project?

Information

What do I already know about grant writing?

What do I want and need to learn about grant writing?

What resources (books, articles, websites, specialists, etc.) can support my efforts to improve my grant writing skills?

Dollars
What skills do I have that would be useful on a grant project?

How much money can I make writing grant proposals?

How much money can I make working part/full-time on a grant-funded project?

What next step will I make to begin getting P-A-I-D to write grants?

What next step will I make to begin getting P-A-I-D as part-time or full-time staff on grant-funded projects?

5.
WEB CONTENT

Tell the Internet who you are.

On September 22, 2010, I started a blog with the goal of offering empowering messages that encourage parents to take charge of life and develop productive families. I called the blog, *I'm Just Sayin'* and published it on Blogger.com—a free blog-publishing service hosted by Google. On the site I wrote family-friendly articles related to education, parenting, home-schooling, holidays—all which related to my reality as a single mother and expertise as a teacher-educator. Each post was written from a personal perspective and concluded with a humorous anecdote or quote, followed by, *I'M JUST SAYIN'!*

As I continued to write, I learned the importance of branding my content. This led me to develop *Man-up Mondays* and *Wellness Wednesdays* on *I'm Just Sayin'*. I paid a freelancer to design logos for both series and set a reminder on my calendar to write posts every week.

I started *Man-up Mondays* on April 28, 2011 to solicit positive stories about good work men were doing in the community. Here's the introductory post:

> **Dr. Bisa Introduces Man-up Mondays:**
> **Shining Light on 'Good' Men**
>
>
>
> I get so tired of hearing that "A good man is hard to find." I beg to differ. I see so many *good* men out there. Please join me in tooting their horns for the entire world to hear!
>
> Rather than piggy-back on negative media—

focusing on what men DON'T do, I want to focus on what men DO. This will be a positive venue to highlight the everyday man who IS doing good things.

What: I will share YOUR stories on men who are manning-up—accepting responsibility and making positive things happen for themselves, their families, and/or the community.

When: Every Monday, starting Monday, May 2, 2011

Where: I'M JUST SAYIN' by Dr. Bisa at www.drbisa.blogspot.com

How: Write an entry of 500 words or less, sharing how the man in your life (significant other, father, brother, friend, co-worker…) is manning-up. Email your Man-up Mondays entry to info@drbisa.com. Be sure to type *Man-up Mondays* in the subject line of the email entry. Please attach his photo to the email. You do NOT have to mention his full name. His first

> name or an alias is fine and understood.
>
> *Maybe these postings will cause men who are slackers to man-up, so women won't have to.*
>
> I'M JUST SAYIN'!

Shortly after starting *Man-up Mondays*, I realized how often I was writing about nutrition. So, I figured I may as well brand all my nutrition recommendations. On May 4, 2011, I started *Wellness Wednesdays* on my blog with the following post:

> I don't know about you, but I have at least three different sizes of clothes in my closet! I can no longer blame it on the boys; they are thirteen and

nine now. It's not baby fat anymore, it's Bisa-fat!

It's time to put up or hush up and lose some weight! Who's with me?

First Lady Michelle Obama is traveling all around the country, in an effort to motivate us to get off our behinds and live healthy lives! She's even doing "The Dougie" and dancing to Beyoncé to encourage our children to get movin'!

I've been sitting around thinking about how I can help. I realized that hundreds of people read my blog every week, so why can't I start by motivating my readers. So, it's on!

Every Wednesday, we will have *Wellness Wednesday*, during which we will discuss ways to live healthy lives, not just diet. We will post a topic each week. Yes, we want you to join in on the conversations. Topics will include nutrition, exercise tips, skin care, oral care, hair care and so much more! If you are a physician or an

> experienced professional on wellness, we welcome you to submit a guest posting at info@drbisa.com.
>
> *My ultimate goal for Wellness Wednesdays is to support my fellow man in being healthy on the inside and out, holistically. Because, if you're ugly on the inside, you're ugly on the outside.*
>
> I'M JUST SAYIN'!

After posting on my blog consistently, at least twice per week, my page views and audience increased. Eventually, I was approached by retail companies requesting to add web links from certain words on my blog to their product websites. I learned this is how many authors monetize their blogs, along with ads. For instance, food, beverage, and health/nutrition companies were very attracted to *Wellness Wednesdays* on my blog. Each time I was contacted by a company about linking their products to my content, I conducted research on the company and their products before making a decision.

Many bloggers monetize their blogs using tools

such as Google AdSense—a program that can automatically display relevant targeted ads on your blog so you can earn income by allowing text matching and ad displays to your site based on your content and visitors. The ads are created and paid for by advertisers who want to promote their products. All bloggers have to do is add to their blogs the text coding Google provides and the earning begins when visitors view or click the linked text. I'm sure you've viewed or clicked on some text that interested you while you were scrolling the internet. Well, someone got paid for your view or click.

My blog, *I'm Just Sayin'*, enabled people I would never meet to discover my talent and read my work. In an effort to support me in expanding my audience and opportunities, my homegirl Jwana sent a message to a public figure she respected and watched daily, in hopes she'd agree to talk with me about my brand and offer some advice. Well, guess what? She answered! Thanks to my ally, Jwana, I was able to schedule a Skype call with René Syler B.K.A. Good Enough Mother.[4]

René Syler co-hosted *The Early Show* on CBS from October 2002 until she left the program in December

---

[4] https://www.goodenoughmother.com/

2006. René shared with me a golden nugget that I will always remember. She told me my website is the wheel and my social media sites are the spokes, so I should focus on making all my content available on my website and share it through posts on social media with links that lead back to my website. Genius! So, after talking with René, I posted to *I'm Just Sayin'* on Blogger.com for the last time on August 11, 2013 and started *Sprinkles of Salt* (#SOS) via the blog feature on my original Dr. Bisa website, which I developed on Vistaprint.com. *Sprinkles of Salt* enabled me to respond to advice-seeking questions I was receiving from my audience about a variety of topics, not just topics related to family, parenting and education. These posts didn't always end with a humorous anecdote or quote, but did conclude with a summary of my advice, followed by *"Sprinkle! Sprinkle."* Get it? Salt… sprinkle.

Here's one of my first posts from August 27, 2013:

#SOS - Help with Doctoral Dissertations

"#SOS, @DrBisa! I am working on my doctoral dissertation. What suggestions do you have?"

First of all, let me just say IGNORE EVERYONE WHO TELLS YOU, "NO ONE WILL EVER READ YOUR DISSERTATION." That's an old saying that started long before the World Wide Web was created. Now that we have the Internet, EVERYONE may have access to your dissertation. Don't believe me? Check out mine, along with UGA Adult Education doctoral graduates over the last decade at: https://athenaeum.libs.uga.edu/handle/10724/26386?show=full.

Another famous saying is "The best dissertation is a done dissertation." I kinda sorta agree with that one. Only because some people try to change the world with their dissertations and never end up getting done due to the complexity of their topics and questions.

My advice is to LISTEN TO YOUR DOCTORAL CHAIRPERSON, assuming you chose a competent chair, that is. I also found one of my professors, who publishes some of the top adult education textbooks and articles, very helpful. World-renowned author, researcher, and UGA professor Dr. Sharan Merriam advised, "You're trying to do too much." She helped me to narrow my focus and decide exactly what I wanted to accomplish in my dissertation. After that, I was on a roll with my writing!

Congratulations to those who are working on the doctoral degree and have reached the dissertation stage! Stay focused and end with a bang! You can save the world in subsequent publications. People will trust your work more, because you'll have "D-r" in front of your name.

Sprinkle! Sprinkle!

After writing web content for my own blog and posting on social media for about three years, I was contacted by Bright Starts/Kids II, one of the top toy companies who manufactures products for babies and young children in the United States, and several other countries. I was told by the staff member they had searched "child development experts" and my name popped up. They were looking to hire an expert to write web content for their products and websites. Following the initial interview call, I was invited onsite to their office in north Atlanta to meet the staff. When I walked in, my name was on a mounted screen with the words, "Welcome, Dr. Bisa Batten Lewis." I wanted to take a picture of the monitor so badly but didn't want to risk looking like an amateur. After a face-to-face interview, I was offered a consulting contract. This was my first contract with a corporation outside of education. It was refreshing to be offered a competitive hourly rate without having to negotiate. They were paying me nearly double what I was making on my average consulting gig with education programs. I loved how they respected me as a professional, posted the web content I wrote for them on their websites, and quoted me accordingly.

Once you gain attention as an expert or a trusted

professional in a particular industry, you will start getting contacted by companies to write web content, but be careful where you attach your name. Having the "Dr." in front of my name has attracted both wanted and unwanted attention. If I had endorsed every product requested, I'd be like the doctor who founded "Your Baby Can Read" and later tried to separate his likeness and image, after the government shut down the company alleging the program had no scientific evidence to make claims and charged it with more than 185 million dollars in fines.

Remind yourself that you are the expert and make efforts to show yourself in the best light online. Remember, once content is published online, it is there to stay. As you consider what you might write on the web, think about the guy who reviewed different types of food on his YouTube channel and caused all the craze for the Patti LaBelle pies. The buzz was all about his delivery of the information for his intended audience, which will vary by industry. Conduct an internet search for topics in your area of expertise and find blogs, products, programs, and services that contain web content that interests you. Think about what you could write to begin capturing the attention of leaders in your profession. No matter what subject you teach, there is web content you could write on a regular basis for a fee or products that would supplement your content via an ad. All you have to do is start exploring and making yourself visible as a specialist or an expert on a particular topic.

As educators, we often get caught up in our own little school bubble and fail to engage with the outside world. Remember, there's a full industry that exists outside of education in the subject you teach. Whether you attend conferences and/or participate in professional organizations, it's essential for you to make connections outside of the school, college or university system, and further engage in industry activities and events related to your subject area. You will be amazed at what you find and how much you already know above the rest, because you teach this subject every day. There are countless readers out there waiting on YOU to write the web content they need to read to achieve their next goal, just as there are countless organizations and companies in need of a content expert like YOU to send them the collection of words they need to publish their next post or promote their latest product.

Now it's time for you to complete the self-work required to get P-A-I-D for writing web content.

SELF-WORK:
Getting P-A-I-D for Writing Web Content

Prospects
What individuals/companies do I know that publish web content in my area of expertise?

What companies do I patronize that need to publish web content?

Allies
Which individuals and groups have capacity to support my goal to write web content?

Information
What do I already know about writing web content?

What do I want and need to learn about writing web content?

What resources can support my efforts to improve web content writing?

Dollars
How much money can I make writing web content in my area of expertise?

What next step will I make to begin getting P-A-I-D to write web content?

6.
ARTICLES

Silent voices won't get heard.

An article is a piece of writing on a particular subject, usually nonfiction, included in a publication. Advancements in technology enable the availability of articles in both print and electronic media, including newspapers, websites, magazines, academic/scientific journals, newsletters, audio recordings (podcasts), blogs, video blogs (vlogs), listicles, academic papers, social media sites, and more. Once you determine the type(s) of articles you want to write, the possibilities are endless. If, writing a book seems too long-term or time-consuming right now, writing articles is a great place to start your authoring journey.

Several years of writing blog posts and earning extra money for them gave me confidence to try my hand at expanding my territory. I joined several professional groups on LinkedIn and started publishing relative content on my page. With LinkedIn considered the leading social media site for professional networking, I was eventually recognized globally as a professional in my field and sought after to write articles for respected publications. I even had to hire a publicist to help me acquire and manage all the opportunities and marketing, which enabled me to write for *Essence* magazine and gave me confidence to submit queries to peer-reviewed journals, such as *The HAAEYC Advocate* and *Exchange* magazine. Through my publicist, I learned there are portals where one can subscribe to receive requests for written content. Once my publicist confirmed my willingness to write based on these requests, she started sending me regular, almost daily, requests to write and send information for articles and publications—to the point I eventually became overwhelmed. The experience showed me my knowledge and expertise were valuable and I had something to say that people wanted to hear.

Even though I had a publicist, I continued to seek

out opportunities on my own because I would remind myself that I know education and the media that are respected in my profession. So, I visited the websites of publications for which I wanted to write. There is usually an author page or Write for Us section on the websites. I followed each of their instructions and contacted the individual noted on the request.

Some will ask for samples of your writing and/or your resume and others won't. Similar to grant writing, all you need to do is follow the individual set of instructions provided by each publication. I was now starting to get paid for writing articles in peer-reviewed journals. It wasn't enough to equal a full-time income, but the money was a great supplement to my income as I fluctuated between teaching full-time and as an adjunct professor at the university level, while working as an independent education consultant and trainer through my own company.

If you were inspired by Chapter One on Editing, you'll be pleased to know that editors are usually assigned to work with authors of journal articles to prepare them to write a quality product for the publication. And if you are inspired by this chapter on Articles, you'll be pleased to know you don't have to go it alone. An editor is often assigned to you during the writing process to support your efforts. When I wrote the article, *I Want My Baby to Read: Supporting Parents in Guiding Early Language and Literacy Development* for *Exchange* magazine[5], I worked one-on-one with an editor for the duration of the process. She reviewed the strategies and recommendations in my article and made sure they were user-friendly and the content flowed well. After several edits, she gave me the thumbs up, confirming the article was ready for review by a larger body, prior to being approved to go to print. So, don't let the article writing or submission process scare you. There is help waiting for you as you get connected!

Writers are useful and necessary in EVERY industry. As an educator, you regularly acquire knowledge related to your subject area to prepare lessons and experiences for students. Writing enables you to document and share some of the research you identify and implement in your classes. No matter what subject you teach, articles are needed to fulfill the primary obligations of educational institutions, socialize individuals into useful members of society, and transmit our cultural values to the next generation.

---

[5] https://www.childcareexchange.com/article/i-want-my-baby-to-read-supporting-parents-in-guiding-early-language-and-literacy-development/5022242/

Review your course content schedule or the list of topics you wrote down at the end of the Research chapter in this book–the one containing all the topics you teach each school year. Now, go online to your preferred search engine and enter "jobs writing articles" to locate requests related to the information you teach students every day. You can narrow your search by entering "jobs writing articles about education" and replace "education" with the subject you teach, are passionate about, or the ones you know best.

You might also consider starting your own personal or business blog. Better yet, you could start a class blog involving your students in publishing articles. There are many free blog sites, similar to blogger.com, including, but not limited to:

WordPress (www.wordpress.org)
Wix (www.wix.com)
Weebly (www.weebly.com)
Tumblr (www.tumblr.com)
Joomla (www.joomla.org)

New free website builders are constantly on the rise, so I recommend conducting a web search for "free website builders" and explore the list of links to see which software program you like most.

Writing on LinkedIn and publishing once or twice per week in groups related to your profession would be a boss move! I can honestly say that many of the opportunities I've had outside of the classroom resulted from articles I'd written and published on LinkedIn. Start with information *you know that you know that you know* without a doubt—those topics you're *voluntold* to share at faculty meetings or present to colleagues on professional development day or at conferences. You can start with an article as simple as "5 Ways to…" You will need to fill in the blank and briefly describe each item on your list. Be sure to include at least one quality resource link to consult, or better yet, a link to your website or blog which would include multiple resources and enable the conversation to continue. People love quick, memorable reads that won't take much of their time while they are scrolling on social media. Remember, you must write and post articles regularly to gain followers and increase viewership. You must also read others' articles in your profession and LinkedIn groups and comment on them regularly. Writing and posting articles while positively engaging with others' articles and posts will increase your integrity, connections and popularity amongst fellow professionals. For your first article, you might consider writing in collaboration with a colleague or two. Then, once you feel confident in your abilities, consider writing as a guest contributor on publications related to your area of expertise. Reach out to authors you respect and ask if you can write a guest post or article with them or for them (with credit going to you, of course). Trust me, most authors who are publishing regularly would love a break from writing, as long as the guest is someone they feel comfortable with connecting. If you are vigilant about engaging with other authors, they will likely invite you to be a guest author for one or more of their articles.

An article doesn't always have to include information from you. It can be a collection of multiple thoughts and opinions. I love these types of opportunities, because they are simply commentaries on particular topics. In 2012, I was honored to be included in an *Essence* magazine article, *How to Enrich Your Child's Education* by Lakeia Brown and Christina M. Tapper.[6] The article consists of information collected from several esteemed education specialists. As a contributor to this article, I was not paid.

---

[6] https://www.essence.com/lifestyle/parenting/how-to-enrich-your-childs-education/

However, I realized there was money in writing and inviting contributors to offer information to bring validity to the content. Contributing content to publications as highly regarded as *Essence* can propel one's career, so I was all in. I love sharing information, so I was honored to participate and be associated with like-minded individuals within the education profession. This one article connected us forever.

So, let's say you want a break from the content you teach and you prefer to write articles related to your personal interests or hobbies. Well, you can do that, too. Honestly, balancing the work you *have* to do with the work you *want* to do will likely increase your ability to grow a particular concept and even start your own business. In 2012, when I was interviewed for a cover story for *Fayette Woman* magazine, I was invited to dinner by one of their writers who also worked as an adjunct instructor at a college. Maggie Worth was so comfortable and confident with her abilities that she didn't write down one word during our interview dinner. We just talked, like girlfriends who went to high school or college together and wanted to catch up. It didn't feel like an interview at all! I walked away wondering what in the heck she was going to write about me, because I didn't feel like she really asked me much. Well, a couple of months later, when the article was released, I couldn't believe how well Maggie understood me and summed up my life! She was gooooood! Read the online version of the article and make your own judgement.[7] After reading the article, ask yourself, is this something you'd like to do—tell others' stories. Today, most of the "news" simply tells stories of what's happening in people's lives. Writers like us are writing and reporting on our fellow man. Instead of having discussions about others amongst your friends or in the breakroom at work, you may as well get PAID to do it.

In 2017, I posted on Facebook a photo of my southern traditional Christmas dinner list while preparing to cook, and a full-blown conversation emerged about how to cook collard greens. My mom and aunt even chimed in offering advice on how to cook good ol' southern collard greens. Two years later, the Facebook user who asked for the advice on how to prepare collards, Maggie Zerkus, another Maggie who works for *Fayette Woman* magazine, reached out to ask if she could write an article featuring our Facebook

---

[7] The Extraordinary Tales of Dr. Bisa Batten Lewis
https://fayettewoman.com/extraordinary-tales-dr-bisa-batten-lewis/

conversation, since "greens are all the jazz right now." Of course, I agreed and followed through with recipes, photos, and responses to all the necessary questions for Maggie to write the article *Facebook Southern Greens* in the November 2019 edition of *Fayette Woman*.[8]

These types of articles are fun, helpful, and uplifting. You might find yourself more amenable to writing about feel-good topics, instead of those related to what you teach or previously taught as an educator. The point is, you get to choose.

If a blog or journal article is an overwhelming start, consider writing articles for a newsletter that relate to the content you teach or administer. Mrs. Burson shared with me that she wrote articles for the textbook publisher's newsletter, where she consulted as an editor. In each book, journal, magazine, or website you read opportunities to get PAID are right in front of you. Some publisher or content editor is waiting on your email request to arrive just in time to fill their next publication. The articles we read don't just fall out of thin air. The ideas are crafted by people like you and me, who have information to contribute—concepts we've thought about in our heads, but realized they

---

[8] https://fayettewoman.com/facebook-southern-greens/

need to be printed. How many ideas have run through your head while you've been reading this book? Are you writing them down? That's step number one—write down your ideas. If you speak and write in more than one language, you might also consider translating articles. I've contracted with education professionals to do both—write articles for a newsletter I administered and/or translate it into a different language for my customers or their customers—usually families. Consider the newsletters you receive monthly or quarterly, no matter how large or small, and determine what topic you'd like to submit as an author for publication. You have to start somewhere and develop your skills from there.

It's time for you to complete the self-work required to get P-A-I-D to write articles.

SELF-WORK:
Getting P-A-I-D for Writing Articles

Prospects
What individuals or companies already publish articles in my area of expertise or interest?

What companies or businesses do I patronize that need to publish articles?

Allies
Which individuals and groups have capacity to support my goal to write articles?

Information
What do I already know about writing articles?

What do I want and need to learn about writing articles?

What resources (books, articles, websites, experts, etc.) can support my efforts to improve article writing?

Dollars
How much money can I make writing articles?

What next step will I make to begin getting P-A-I-D to write articles?

Part III:
Getting P-A-I-D for Speaking

7.
PRESENTING

Put your talents on display.

Growing up in a southern Baptist church, where my grandfather was Pastor, an average height, thin man who we called "Big Daddy," forced me into an early start performing in front of people. Whether we were singing in the choir, reporting what we learned in Sunday School, or reciting our Easter speeches, presenting became the norm for me. As a matter of fact, I wish more churches would revert to allowing youth to report on what they learned in Sunday School or Children's Church, so they could gain experience speaking in front of crowds. That's what happened with me. Church is where I gained the confidence to present.

In addition to recognizing my gift to write, Mrs. Suttles, my seventh grade English teacher, nurtured my gift to speak. Around 1985, I performed Langston Hughes' *Still Here* for our Black History Month assignment in her class. I walked in front of the classroom limping and humped over with my lip hanging and mouth twisted, and recited slowly in an elderly, submissive-sounding dialect:

> *"I been scarred and battered.*
> *My hopes the wind done scattered.*
> *Snow has friz me, sun has baked me.*
>
> *Looks like between 'em, they done*
> *tried to make me stop laughin',*
> *stop lovin', stop livin'.*
> *But I don't care! I'm still here!"*

After my performance, I received a rousing round of applause from our classroom teachers, Mrs. Suttles and Mrs. Alford, and my peers. For the remainder of the week, Mrs. Suttles requested her colleagues allow me to recite the poem to their classes. I tell you, I must have performed that poem a dozen times. Each time, I made it more dramatic, and even started to play around with the words by changing "has" to "is" or "done" to enhance the effect. From that point on, speaking in front of crowds became a passion.

Throughout my youth and early adulthood, I entered beauty pageants and either sang, recited a poem, or presented a monologue. Just like I did with Langston Hughes's poem, I found different ways to wow the crowd. For instance, during pageant introductions, I'd say hello in several languages to set myself apart from the other contestants. I'm proud to say it worked as I was crowned queen in at least half the pageants I entered. Thank you Big Daddy and Mrs. Suttles!

As educators, we are required to participate in professional development several times per year. While you were sitting in those sessions, have you ever envisioned yourself being the speaker in front of the crowd? Have you ever wondered what it felt like? At the end of the training, did you ever think or say to yourself, "I could've done that" or "He didn't teach me anything I didn't already know"? Well, my friend, you should consider getting P-A-I-D for presenting.

Due to the success of our SIP and YTA grant projects, even in their early stages, the Dean of the ASU

College of Education, Dr. Claude Perkins and I were approved to present the programs at a conference in Toronto, Canada in 2001. Not only was this my very first time traveling by air, but I was six months pregnant with my second son. During the trip, I met education faculty from all over the world who were supplementing their income in a variety of ways, including presentations. Interestingly, this was the first time I can recall presenting in front of such a large, diverse group of experienced education professionals. Dr. Perkins' presence made me feel more comfortable. Therefore, I recommend collaborating with at least one colleague to conduct your first presentation. You might even team up to take your presentation on the road. At some point, you will feel more comfortable presenting by yourself.

No matter how you start presenting, alone, as a duo, or as a group, you don't have to know answers to all the questions. Start by presenting on a lesson or topic you know well and be sure to provide opportunities for participants to collaborate on an intentional activity and share their ideas. Here is an outline of one of my presentations. Use it as a starting point and build from there. I use this format to write instructional plans for my workshops and speeches. I merely tweak the format based on the audience, goal of the session, and allotted time.

Dr. Bisa's Presentation Outline

I. Introduction
II. Instructional Plan

Objective	What participants will do
Content	Slides, materials, and handouts
Procedures	Discussions and application activity
Allotted Time	How long each step in the procedures will last

III. Wrap-up (Closing Activity and Q&A)
IV. Assessment of Learning Outcomes

Based on the length of the presentation, I repeat the Instructional Plan to construct the delivery of content and activities for each objective. If you're seeking to offer credit for your presentations, such as state-approved training hours, Professional Learning Units (PLUs), or Continuing Education Units (CEUs), each approval process will require a particular set of information for submission. The requirements should be available on the website related to the particular type of credits professionals need in your field.

In 2001, I participated in an early education Training for Trainers (TFT) course to become a state-approved trainer in Georgia, which enables me to offer creditable workshops for early educators. I have a state-approved trainer code and each training I present must be approved by the Georgia Professional Development System for Early Educators. Every training I offer for early educators has a training code, Workforce Knowledge & Competency number, and training expiration date. I must renew my trainer approval status, as well as update each training and resubmit for approval, every five years. When I worked as a full-time educator, I started by only scheduling at least one training on Saturday of each month or two evening trainings over the course of a month. During the Training for Trainers course, I learned our state had fourteen Child Care Resource and Referral Agencies (CCR&Rs) who were primarily state-funded and held professional development for childcare providers throughout each month. I connected with our local CCR&R—yep, just popped up one day with my resume and lists of state-approved trainings, and my training journey began. A "Super Saturday," which generally included six hours of state-approved training for registered participants, would add an additional $450-$900 to my income for the month—just for that one day. One two-hour training in the evening on a weekday, which was usually held from 7-9 PM, after childcare centers closed, would yield an additional $150-$300 per month. If I was able to book two evening trainings, the amount would double to $300-$600. The amount of pay was based on the event and how it was funded. As a newbie, I accepted what was offered. I didn't feel experienced enough to negotiate a higher rate. Through volunteering and networking, I was eventually able to build up my reputation to the point where I had to turn down opportunities because I became exhausted from working full-time for eight or more hours each day and working late into the evening with only one day of rest on the weekend. As I continued to engage in community service by joining professional organizations and serving on education boards and committees of community organizations, my network expanded to the point where I started meeting the giants in my field. I will never forget meeting one veteran presenter/trainer at an invite-only consortium. I noticed her repeatedly looking at me from an adjacent table—in a curious, observatory manner, but not saying anything. At the end of the event, we introduced ourselves to one another although, both of our reputations preceded us. She said, "I was told I needed to meet you. I replied to the person who told me that, 'No, she needs to meet ME.'" We both laughed and became close friends. I consider her one of my treasured mentors. She taught me how to extend my reach and avoid turning down opportunities by hiring fellow colleagues to work when I can't or don't want to. Her advice enabled me to expand my business and support fellow colleagues, all at once.

In 2006, I was reminded of my goal to become my own boss within five years of starting my consulting and training company. I reached out to one of my allies *(A)*—Dr. Anita Smith, Faculty in the Department of Child and Family Development and Senior Public Service Associate (*Retired*) at the University of Georgia. She administered the Georgia CDA Initiative—a grant-funded project enabling early educators to earn the national Child Development Associate (CDA) Credential, awarded by the Council for Professional Recognition in Washington, DC. I met Anita in 2002 at a "Better Brains for Babies" Train-the-Trainer in

Macon, Georgia through Amy Hough-Simmon, who was the Training Approval Coordinator for the State. I called Anita and shared with her my goal of working for myself as a full-time ECE consultant and trainer. Because Anita and Amy had both mentored me on how to appropriately conduct a high-quality CDA training course, and Anita and I had collaborated on offering several courses and CDA Advisor Trainings in South Georgia, Anita was confident I was ready to strike out on my own. The timing was perfect, because Anita's grant project at UGA had just received grant funding for three community CDA courses at $1200 per participant. Anita was intentional about holding many of the trainings in rural areas, where there's a lack of access to quality professional development, which affects the quality of early learning experiences and brain development for young children. Living in Albany, Georgia, near many rural areas in southwest Georgia, I was contracted to conduct two of the three CDA courses. The rest is history. Our limit was twenty participants per class, which enabled us to maintain instructional quality. I still apply that same rule today—quality over quantity. While some trainers will pack a room, which in turn packs their pockets, the quality of the experience is likely reduced due to the challenge of implementing engaging activities and protocols. While some trainers may have mastered the ability to engage large audiences during training, it should not be a general practice. There's a major difference between a training and a seminar. In the case of providing quality training, "the more the merrier" is not a good practice.

Once funding for the Georgia CDA Initiative ended, Anita gave the CDA instructors she'd mentored permission to continue training at the level of quality initiated through the project and utilize the materials that were developed. Much of the time I've been able to supplement and even replace my teaching income has been due to the offering CDA training for early educators, which is one of the required credentials for childcare providers in the ECE profession. Collecting $1200 from childcare providers, who are already far underpaid, is quite a challenge—even when the payments are broken into increments over the duration of the course, which can last as long as six months. Therefore, I primarily collaborate with community organizations who fully fund the CDA course for participants, just like Anita's program. Through community advocates and grant-funded organizations, such as United Way of Greater Atlanta, YMCA,

YWCA and Head Start, my company is able to continue offering CDA courses at no cost to participants. As a community advocate myself, I offer the course at a reduced rate and ensure the quality is not affected. Even though I've been conducting CDA training for nearly twenty years and have updated my course multiple times, I continue to give credit for course development in my CDA course syllabus to Dr. Anita Smith and her UGA Georgia CDA Initiative because she shared her "baby" with me in hopes the standard of quality would continue to spread far and wide—transcending her funding proposals and noteworthy career.

As you become a master at presenting, expand your territory and diversify opportunities. Think of all the presenters you've listened to in various settings and picture yourself on those very stages or at the front of those same rooms. If I told you how much money presenters often make, you'd be angry and maybe even intrigued. Okay, you twisted my arm so I'll tell you—well, kinda. Can you believe many of the presenters who come to your school or to a district event to inspire, motivate, and/or train educators often score no less than $10,000 per appearance? If the contract includes multiple appearances and/or consulting during a chosen school year, that $10,000 multiplies. College faculty and "education experts" (former educators) are making BIG bucks consulting with and presenting for schools and school districts.

Every profession usually requires creditable professional development. Find out which agency or organization regulates required credentials and certifications in your profession and enroll in any train-the-trainer courses they offer. You'd likely be a great candidate to learn how to teach those courses. This is another benefit of joining professional organizations as you have regular opportunities to network and learn. Once you start crafting each of your presentations, you will become a pro and get excited about improving your instructional practices. My rule is: *If I'm bored with the instructional plan, the participants will be bored during my presentation.* To prepare a successful presentation, put yourself in the place of the participants who will be on the receiving end and plan a session or training from which they will learn beneficial information and recommendations tailored to their professional needs, while enjoying the experience.

Now, it's time for you to complete the self-work required to get P-A-I-D to present.

SELF-WORK:
Getting P-A-I-D for Presenting

Prospects
What individuals or companies do I know that already utilize presenters in my area of expertise?

What companies, schools, agencies, or businesses do I patronize that need presenters?

Allies
Which individuals and groups have capacities to support my goal to present?

Information
What do I already know about presenting and what do I want and need to learn about presenting?

What resources (books, articles, websites, experts, etc.) can support my efforts to improve presentation skills?

Dollars
How much money can I make presenting?

What next step will I make to begin getting P-A-I-D to present?

8.
CONSULTING

*Go to the water and drink and be okay
with making the trip alone!*

In 1999, after being fed-up with the pressures of standardized testing fueled by subtle nudges for all students to pass by any means necessary, instead of packing up my first-grade classroom for the summer, I decided to pack my car. Shortly after my decision to say "so long" to public education the first time, I was hired by my Alma Mater, Albany State University, as an Early Childhood Education Instructor. Since 1998, I'd been teaching in the evenings as an adjunct instructor at Albany Technical College, so I was excited to be offered a full-time opportunity to work with adult learners; even though, I was pretty close to their age and sometimes younger.

In the year 2000, as I slowly learned about the additional income some of my colleagues at the university were making on the side, I decided to start my own education consulting business as a side hustle. I named it Ideal Consultants. I later changed the company to a limited liability corporation, based on advice from my accountant, and named the company Ideal Early Learning, LLC, a service company devoted to providing quality technical assistance and professional development for early education programs and schools, in an effort to meet the growing need for more proficient early educators. It is the mission of Ideal Early Learning, LLC to provide early care and education practitioners the necessary knowledge and skill enhancements to appropriately guide tomorrow's leaders.

When I first started consulting, which primarily involved training childcare providers, my contracts ranged from $75-$150/hour. Aside from conducting training for early educators and administrators, which I discussed in the chapter on presenting, I started providing technical assistance—on-site services to assess and support early learning centers in improving program quality to reach a chosen quality benchmark up to national accreditation. I had to participate in professional development to learn how to use industry assessment and evaluation tools, such as the *Infant and Toddler Environment Rating Scale (ITERS), Early Childhood Environment Rating Scale (ECERS), Teaching Pyramid Infant–Toddler Observation Scale (TPITOS),* and the *Classroom Assessment Scoring System (CLASS®).* Once I learned how to conduct observations and assessments using the instruments contractors requested, which were generally all the same, I became more confident in my role as a technical assistance consultant and could choose geographic locations where I wanted to consult. Contracts would vary from client to client, but primarily required at least one three- to four-hour site visit to childcare centers or elementary schools each month documented by a technical assistance report on an approved form for the specified project. As you research to find out which *prospects (P's)* in your industry need consultants to conduct site visits, program reviews, assessments/evaluations and performance reports, your jaw may drop when you learn *information (I)* about the contracts. See, I likely made money on the low end consulting in child care centers, but made at least double when consulting with corporations and grade-level schools. Based on your level of expertise, I recommend starting with smaller companies or schools and seeking larger clients as your skills advance.

One of my favorite consulting contracts was with Georgia Public Broadcasting/PBS Kids. There were seven of us from around the state who were hired as Ready to Learn Consultants through a literacy project primarily funded by the U.S. Department of Education with the goal of teaching parents and educators how to utilize smart TV to teach literacy skills to children. We were provided award-winning children's books, plush animals and toys from all the TV shows that aired on PBS Kids, and printed materials created by the program to distribute to workshop participants. We used clips and excerpts from books and shows, such as *Clifford: The Big Red Dog* to teach literacy through character education. Every episode involved some lesson being learned related to character. Have you ever noticed that the dogs bark around humans and only talk when they are with other dogs? Or, did you realize the voice of "Caillou" was a girl? She passed away in 2003 and left quite the legacy. The real-life situations Caillou experienced provided many talking points and meaningful conversations with parents. I felt privileged knowing the inside scoop on the shows and sharing those we could with parents and educators. We were able to provide Ready to Learn literacy trainings all over Georgia at no cost to participants. This was a dream contract! How did I get this awesome consulting gig? Well, I must tell you the importance of minding your behavior everywhere you go; because, you never know who's watching you and the opportunities that can result from positive connections with people. It's possible to have countless *allies (A's)*, if you genuinely play your cards right. I don't even recall where I first met Kathy McCollister, who was the sole Ready to Learn Consultant for quite some time, but she remembered me and recommended my name to Laura Miller who was administering the Read to Learn project at Georgia Public Broadcasting. I was honored to be noticed and recommended by someone as highly regarded as Kathy. She is considered a veteran in my profession. At the time Kathy recommended me as a Ready to Learn Consultant, I was still living in Albany, GA—271 miles from the city of Atlanta where the Georgia Public Broadcasting offices were located. Because I knew I had to drive to take advantage of opportunities as they were afforded, I had no problem jumping in my vehicle and riding to Atlanta, usually alone, to participate in meetings, workshops, and conferences while building my reputation and career. You never know how or when your blessings are going to come. You just have to be ready to accept them. You've heard the saying, "Be ye also ready."

All educators should consider their favorite networks, television shows and movies and the types of consultants who are required to support them. You don't think all the sitcoms, soap operas, and dramas with medical scenes, throughout the years, were successful without hiring medical consultants to ensure the accuracy of facts, gestures, and language, do you? Movies like *Daddy Day Care* and Disney/Pixar's *Inside Out* are filled with information likely provided by early education experts. I would have loved one of those consulting contracts! What are your favorite television shows related to your profession that clearly hire consultants to work with the writers and producers to ensure the content and context align with reality in the profession? Your favorite TV show or movie could be one of your *prospects (P's)*.

In 2016, I returned to the public school system, after learning high schools across the country were offering early childhood education career pathways in their Career and Technical Education (CTE) programs. The ECE pathway is much different from traditional child development, Family and Consumer Sciences, or Home Economics courses many of us took in middle or high school. The programs focus on preparing students for the workforce. Once I learned about the opportunity to train high school students to work with young children, which many of them were already doing at home anyway, I jumped at the chance.

On Friday, August 5, 2016, I reported for new employee orientation at the district office as an Early Childhood Education Instructor. The first day of school was the following Monday—the next workday. After not working in the school system for seventeen years and not working a full-time job in six years, I knew I was in for a challenge. Aside from the shock of being back in the classroom and with teenagers all day for the first time, I was a bit doubtful. Instead of wallowing in my own insecurities, I took off my entrepreneurial hat and put on my teacher vest to get the job done.

Although I had to present a keynote at a conference on Saturday, the day after my orientation, I jetted down the interstate to the teacher supply store and then out to the high school to decorate my bulletin boards and prepare my classroom for students. During my first week, I barely thought I'd make it through the full school year, especially since technology had changed, cell phones had become a staple of the teen wardrobe, and parent involvement was the opposite of what I was used to when teaching first graders nearly two decades before. As the year went on and students realized I was firm, fair and consistent, plus more importantly, I cared about them, my six classes containing over 150 total students became extensions of my immediate family. I, surprisingly, renewed my contract for the next school year and ended up working full-time as a high school CTE instructor teaching ECE for *three years*. Both the school and the district respected and appreciated my work and willingness to share my expertise with fellow colleagues. I was named the Early Childhood Education Career Pathway Lead at the district level and the CTE Lead Teacher for the Health Sciences and Human Services Academy at the high school.

Staying for three years enabled me to support the high school and the district in upgrading the ECE career pathway to industry standards and implementing the national Child Development Associate (CDA) program, which I'd been training early educators on for nearly twenty years. I was happy with my salary, which was handsomely based on my education and experience, and had planned to hang around for a while, until I started to feel the stresses commonly felt by full-time educators. I'd been lied on by students, cursed out by parents, and didn't feel safe anymore, especially after colleagues' classroom relocations solely left my classroom on a hall by itself next to the only outside door that was opened on our floor during transitions. In a school with over 3,000 students and one-third of them having to walk by several times each day, as I stood by my classroom door, I became no stranger to anxiety. The rise in school shootings around the nation didn't help. How does this experience relate to consulting? Well, after questioning myself about whether or not I should continue working in the school system earning "good money" and feeling secure with those "good benefits," I realized the new possibilities before me. Although I'd experienced somewhat of a celebrity status in my profession, prior to returning to the school system, I'd taken my full-time teaching position seriously and gave 100% effort to my school and the district. I participated in professional development, whether it was required or not, and spent most of my summers leading and learning amongst colleagues. Those three years in the classroom and stepping up as a teacher-leader prepared me to refresh my professional skills and become familiar with new territory. I learned a lot about CTE and recognized gaps I am charged to fill for school districts across the nation, as I am contracted to provide consultation on how to implement quality ECE programs, the "academy school" concept, career pathways, and the High School CDA Program. I met some amazing colleagues during my three years teaching at the high school and remain connected. Actually, the reason I decided to write this book is based on conversations I tried to have during lunch with fellow co-workers in the breakroom. I want every educator out there to be paid more money, no matter what their salary may be. We have the ability to pay ourselves!

Don't sell yourself short or count yourself out. You know what you know and do well in your industry. Find prospects who can use someone with your knowledge and expertise. Once I became a seasoned, diversely experienced education professional, I was able to charge based on my worth. As I mentioned in the previous chapter on Presenting, there are consultants who make tens of thousands of dollars on one consulting contract with one school in a single school year. Once you make a name for yourself and improve your reputation, you can enjoy the same benefits.

Now, it's time for you to complete the self-work required to get P-A-I-D to consult.

SELF-WORK:
Getting P-A-I-D for Consulting

Prospects
What individuals or companies already utilize consultants in my area of expertise?

What companies or businesses do I patronize that need consultants?

On what topics or needs could I consult?

Allies
Which individuals and groups have capacity to support my goal to consult?

Information
What do I already know about consulting?

What do I want and need to learn about consulting?

What resources (books, articles, websites, experts, etc.) can support my efforts to improve my consulting skills?

Dollars
How much money can I make consulting in my area of expertise?

What next step will I make to begin getting P-A-I-D to consult?

Part IV:
Getting P-A-I-D for Selling

9.
PRODUCTS

If you can't find one, create it.

As educators, we are constantly creating different types of media to help our students learn the content we teach. Whether it's a twist to an alphabet song, a counting song, a rap or poem for memorizing a math formula or sequence of historic events, we educators are some of the most undercelebrated artists in the world. And, why is that? It's because we rarely publish or monetize our work. Have you ever written a

poem, song, or other type of art for the benefit of helping your students to learn? What did you do with the work you created? Well, it's time for you to dig it up and figure out how you can get P-A-I-D selling your creation to the world.

In the early 2000's, I was training early educators and parents on appropriate strategies for potty training their toddlers, when I realized how difficult it was to find a suitable children's book to appropriately demonstrate the process. So, I did what any self-respecting writer would do. I wrote my own.

Let's Potty was published in 2006. I found a publisher in the Atlanta area who provided a hands-on approach. At the time, I was working as Director of Instruction for the Division of Early Care and Education and Academic Programs at Albany Technical College, which was housed in a separate building on campus and encompassed a child development center. The signature style of the illustrator who worked on the project, was creating characters from pictures of real children. My youngest son was enrolled in the toddler classroom at the child development center on campus, so I recommended we include him and a couple of children whose parents either worked at the center or were close friends. The publisher drove down to Albany take the pictures of the children in various settings needed in the book and the project proceeded from there. After several edits, the book was published. I wanted to ensure the illustrations in the book were diverse, since children of every ethnicity use the toilet. The book was printed as a high-quality board book and turned out to be very successful, especially in Japan.

I was able to increase my income by coupling presentations with book signings at community events and professional conferences. If you haven't written a children's book, I highly recommend you look into it; because, color printing is not nearly as expensive anymore. With so many publishing options available, the experience is likely to be much smoother than for those of us who were publishing before Amazon KDP, Book Baby, Lightning Source and other competitors. As long as you save all your files electronically, you can print and bound almost anything. When Our Rainbow Press published *Let's Potty*, they distributed it in Barnes and Noble, Amazon, and any place books were sold. I maintain rights to the book and currently sell it as well. This was a great deal for a new author who didn't have to invest a dime in illustrating or publishing the book. All the money I make from selling the book is 100 percent profit.

WINGS Curriculum

After training current and prospective educators for over eight years, my work began to feel fragmented because I was only providing the services I was contracted to deliver. There was so much more educators needed to know and wanted to learn. I felt the need to remain connected with all of them and coach them on the topics I wasn't contracted to train them on. It was clear that these two to six-hour workshops were not enough to bring change to participants' classrooms.

In 2008, I started compiling all the workshops and handouts I'd created relating to the daily curriculum in early learning classrooms, including assessment, evaluation, lesson planning, developmentally and culturally appropriate practices, special needs/inclusion, and anything else I'd developed to advance best practices for child development and learning. My goal was to somehow put all of these practices together in an organized format, so that if I only got to train a group of teachers once or twice, or better yet, if I never got to train them at all, they would still be able to plan and implement quality learning experiences for young children on a daily basis—anytime and anywhere. Well, *WINGS: The Ideal Curriculum for Children in Preschool* was born in the summer of 2009.

Unsure of how to develop a curriculum, I contacted a local curriculum company who produced a very successful and lucrative character education curriculum. Mr. Elbert and Mrs. Thelma Solomon of *I Care* Curriculum, lived only thirty-five minutes outside of Albany and were eager to guide me on this journey—for a very fair fee. I will never forget our first call, when Mr. Solomon asked me if I already had a graphic designer. I was so green I didn't even know I needed one. Once the Solomons realized how much I didn't know and needed to learn, as well as my modest finances, they set me up on a business contract allowing the payment of reduced monthly fees through the completion of the project. There were a couple of months when I didn't have the money and they granted me extensions. The Solomons were my allies and true Godsends.

After WINGS Curriculum was published, they even promoted it on their website, with their clients, and invited me to exhibit at their conferences. WINGS Curriculum and *I Care* Curriculum complemented each other, rather than conflicting or competing, so this arrangement was the perfect partnership.

With clients in nearly thirty states, WINGS Curriculum is making a difference in the early education profession and has been supplementing my income for a decade. I love being able to employ colleagues to conduct training on the curriculum and make a percentage of sales. Our Monthly Lesson Plan Ideas and downloadable fillable forms from our Spread MyWINGS Online Resource Center are the most beloved products in the WINGS Curriculum learning system. I look forward to introducing even more products to simplify early educators' work with children, while appropriately meeting their developmental needs. I also look forward to employing more colleagues.

As you explore your own product ideas, check out WINGS Curriculum at wingscurriculum.com. *Let's Potty* is available on the WINGS website[9].

Singing Up A Buzz
After I created WINGS Curriculum, I realized each thematic unit needed a song to support early educators in implementing the content for each month. I was already writing new songs for each of the three sets of Monthly Lesson Plan Ideas—infants, toddlers, and preschoolers. Finally, five years after I started writing WINGS Curriculum, I gathered the resources to write, produce, record, and publish a children's music CD with one song aligned with each thematic unit of the curriculum. In 2013, *Singing Up a Buzz* was released and distributed.

---

[9] wingscurriculum.com/product/lets-potty

I moved to Atlanta in 2008, which placed me in the vicinity of the resources I needed to reach many of my goals. Living on the south side of Atlanta in one of the suburban areas where celebrities like to lay low and focus on their families, I was able to connect with a veteran singer/songwriter/producer. My friend Denise introduced me to "Miss Kay," a trusted friend of Kandi Burruss, who was starting her own music production company. You might know Kandi from the hit R&B group Xscape, an accomplished singer, songwriter and businesswoman in her own right. Kandi and I shared a couple of mutual friends and at the time, my youngest son and her daughter attended the same elementary school. Miss Kay took me on as a client and I was able to record in a studio on one of Kandi's properties. Because I wasn't a true singer, I felt too intimidated to record at the Kandi Factory.

My son, Jordan, was able to participate in the project, for a fee of course, whenever we needed children's voices. After researching various publishing platforms, I settled on publishing and distributing the music with CD Baby. We were very proud of the *Singing Up a Buzz* CD and quickly sold out of hard copies. The music is still available on major digital platforms. You can listen to snippets of each song and make purchases[10]. In addition to the fee I paid my son to record in the studio, I paid him a portion of every CD sale. Although my oldest son chose not to sing on the CD, this was a teachable moment in entrepreneurship for my entire family.

My good friend, Angela Russ-Ayon, is an award-winning early childhood music producer, author, keynote speaker, and trainer. We met through one of the founders of the company who published our first children's books. Long before I met Angela, whose reputation preceded her, she was making big bucks creating and selling products, primarily related to health and wellness, music and movement, and child development. Although Angela has a business degree, she's been able to parlay her life's work into a successful career in early education and health and wellness. Whether she is keynoting or exhibiting at a conference or event, her products are sold all over the world. Having so many products to choose from with different themes enables Angela to be booked at a variety of events in multiple professions. Producers like her are able to get paid well for both presenting and exhibiting at the same event. She has mastered this concept and I

---

[10] The main website for Singing Up a Buzz is store.cdbaby.com/cd/drbisabattenlewis

respectfully consult her for ideas on maximizing opportunities to simultaneously showcase presentations and products. Check out Angela's products and presentations at abridgeclub.com. I often incorporate her children's books and music into my presentations. We reciprocally send business each other's way. I'm honored to have such a highly regarded artist as my A-*ally*!

The launch of entrepreneurial websites allowing teachers to sell products they create, such as Teachers Pay Teachers (TpT), has enabled educators to quit, retire, or make a heck of a salary supplement. Some teachers have even become millionaires, simply by selling products they created to support the children in their classrooms and continuing to increase production from there.

Whether you want to become a millionaire like TpT Top Seller Rachel Lynette, who earned over two million dollars in 2014, earn $50,000 like nearly 200 fellow educators, or bring in a few hundred dollars per month, you can significantly increase your salary and enhance your style of living by uploading your products to TpT. I've had my products on there for quite some time and get emails several times per week showing I've sold products I uploaded over three YEARS ago. I rarely even log onto TpT for months at a time, but my products are available 24/7 and sales are automatically made through the website without any additional effort on my part. It's easy money when technology is used that you don't have to babysit. Are there any websites where you purchase ideas, templates, and/or forms? Consider becoming a seller on those same websites, instead of merely a customer. You can start with one idea and increase from there. Explore the TpT Blog to get your wheels turning.[11] I know you've got some cool handouts, worksheets, templates and/or forms you created for your classroom. Stop sharing them on social media or via email for free and start getting PAID for the works of art you create.

What if creating products is not your thing? That's perfectly fine! Many educators or former educators are able to earn good money selling *other people's* products. Consider textbook sales, learning materials, equipment related to your particular area of expertise, and on and on. You can either purchase the products wholesale and sell them at a formalized retail rate, or you can sell the products on your website and the author or creator ship them on your behalf. You would never have to house

---

[11] blog.teacherspayteachers.com

inventory or worry about being out of stock. Believe it or not, this is what catalog companies often do. They include products on their websites and in their catalogs that they know their clientele would want, and they make BIG money selling those products. They usually have no hand in creating any of the products. They only make money from selling them.

The next time you go to a professional conference, spend some time in the exhibit hall scouting around for products you like. Take notice of those with which you want to be associated. Ask the exhibitors questions that will help you understand the business side of selling those products. Don't be too pushy but let the select few know, who you will intentionally choose, that you have used or highly respect the quality of the product and want to explore how you might *officially* share them with fellow education professionals and schools. You might add that you already recommend their products all the time. However, you feel at a loss for information and have even wondered if opportunities are available for product training or whether you should consider exploring marketing or consulting with the company to extend your knowledge (definitely slip that in). If you are strategic and only ask questions after you've shown genuine interest in the company's mission and products, you might score yourself a consulting gig and possibly, a new career.

If you create products and want to increase sales by offering them in a catalog, plan ahead for conferences by visiting the website to see which exhibitors are participating and schedule meetings to pitch your products. During conferences, countless meetings are held, especially in the exhibit hall. After I wrote WINGS Curriculum and got it off the ground, my next goal was to have it sold in a well-known catalog of early learning classroom products. In November 2010, my session proposal was approved to present at the National Association for the Education of Young Children (NAEYC) Annual Conference in Anaheim, California, in addition to a joint presentation with a colleague from United Way of Greater Atlanta. Even though WINGS Curriculum was only a year young, I contacted three early learning catalog companies. I knew all of them would be exhibiting at the conference, because the NAEYC Annual Conference is the largest attended early childhood education event. I went to their websites and made contact with the appropriate individuals listed on their staff page. In every single case, I was able to reach the right individual, even if I had to be referred by the staff member I initially contacted. During the conference, I held meetings with all three of the chosen catalog companies and not long after the conference, signed an exclusive sales agreement with one of the top catalog companies in my profession. I accomplished this by visiting websites and sending emails to make connections and you can do the same. Seeing WINGS Curriculum in a quality catalog and on the company's website was a DREAM accompanied by some FAT checks!

Now, it's time for you to complete the self-work required to get P-A-I-D to sell products.

SELF-WORK:
Getting P-A-I-D for Selling Products

Prospects
What products are necessary in my area of expertise and which of those products can I create to fill gaps in my area of expertise?

What businesses would purchase my products?

Which companies or individuals sell products I would market?

Allies
Which individuals and groups have capacity to support my goal to create or sell products?

Information
What do I already know about selling products and what do I want and need to learn about selling products?

What resources can support my efforts to improve my sales skills?

Dollars
How much money can I make selling products?

What next step will I make to begin getting P-A-I-D to sell products?

10.
PERFORMANCES

Blessings come in many colors.

One of my undergrad professors bravely shared a story about a major opportunity she missed that sparked my curiosity about all the different *prospects* we fail to consider as educators. As she discussed her successful experiences working in and out of the classroom, she shared the story of how she turned down the opportunity to consult on a children's television show based on a singing purple dinosaur, because she thought it was weird and wouldn't catch on. I will never forget that story. She reflected on how adamant she was when explaining how the concept would never work. Our eyes and mouths opened wide with everyone looking around at each other in disbelief. This was a time when the purple dinosaur was at the height of his career, so everyone knew exactly who she was talking about. What I learned from her experience is there are opportunities for educators to make money in other industries, including television and film. I can only imagine how much the person(s) inside the purple dinosaur suit made for every episode and performance. Hmmm…

In 2011, I received direct messages on my social media accounts and a voicemail on my business phone from the casting producer of a new television show being created by Shed Media, the UK creator and distributor of drama, factual, documentary, reality, and historical television content who was purchased by Warner Brothers Entertainment Company. This new show was called "America's Supernanny"—a spinoff from their previous British hit show "Supernanny." They wanted me to audition. The casting producer had even reached out to my former publicist, who was anxious to step back into her role and work with me again. Once I confirmed the call was real, I returned the casting producer's call. From that point on, the ball started rolling extremely fast. I had a phone conference, followed by a Skype interview, which lead to my being chosen as a finalist and being flown to Burbank, California for a screentest. I had to sign my contract ahead of time to accept the role, in advance of being chosen, which included salary, promotional appearances, work schedule, and more. All this happened within five days from when I first returned the casting producer's call. I quickly learned the reality of the television industry saying, "Hurry up and wait."

Upon arriving to the airport in Burbank, I was met by a production assistant who transported me to a beautiful boutique hotel and coached me on what to expect. During the three or four days I was in California, I was engaged in several in-person interviews at Warner Brothers and a screentest that involved my being placed in a family's home for several hours to resolve the challenges they had with their young sons. My experiences as an early educator came into full effect, and I was able to resolve the family's concerns from potty training, sleeping arrangements, eating preferences, and interpersonal skills. Fast forward several weeks later, I followed up on the role and learned Deborah Tillman, a published author and child care center owner from Virginia, had been chosen as America's Supernanny. In this case, having a doctoral degree worked against me, but I learned even more about opportunities available for educators. I was disappointed to learn how much actresses often make in their initial contracts. I assumed the role would pay six figures, but I was sadly mistaken. My research and inquiries revealed that actresses were making less than $30/hour and roughly $50,000 for an eight to ten-episode season. My offer exceeded the average rate but was far less than I was already paying myself as an education consultant and trainer. For this reason, I was not as disappointed at not being chosen for the role. However, don't get it twisted. I'd love to have another opportunity to perform on television.

No matter which subject you teach, your industry relies on performances in a variety of ways, on and off television. For instance, every industry holds professional conferences and hires special talent to come in to perform for participants. In early childhood education, we often hire performers of children's music to present workshops and keynotes or provide brain breaks. Interestingly, these performers, whether credentialed or not, usually get paid more than the speakers who are published authors with advanced degrees.

When I wrote and published my *Singing Up a Buzz* music CD, this was my rationale. I was tired of watching performers, who sometimes had no credentials, make thousands of dollars for presenting a 30-minute keynote and selling their music CDs and/or books immediately after, while I was either brought in as a volunteer presenter or paid well under $1,000 for presenting research-based best practices for a whole six-hour day. I knew I didn't want to be booked as a singer or entertainer; I just wanted the opportunity to use my own music in my curriculum and presentations. However, if singing were really my passion, I'd perform songs from *Singing Up a Buzz* without hesitation.

There are many performers in education that are somewhat average but are paid very well, especially in early childhood education. Largely because children are so forgiving. When a performer creates products or is featured on products that sell well, they get booked more frequently. Therefore, products and performing can go hand-in-hand if the producer is open to performing. Actually, there are producers who consult with others to perform on their behalf, especially when they are in high demand. Just as I hire consultants to present workshops, unless I'm explicitly requested, performers may duplicate, and sometimes multiplicate, themselves to fulfill all the bookings coming their way.

I have realized the value of performers in all

industries and hope you will, too. Whether you are an English/Language Arts teacher who can romantically or subliminally recite poetry, an art teacher who can draw impressive cartoon figures or still life, a math teacher who has created unique songs or rhymes as pneumonic devices for remembering formulas, or a social studies teacher who has employed astounding strategies to make history sound interesting, there's a myriad of professional performances to supplement or replace your teaching income. For music, chorus, and band teachers, your options for getting P-A-I-D for performing are ENDLESS!

Now, it's time for you to complete the self-work required to get P-A-I-D to perform.

SELF-WORK:
Getting P-A-I-D for Performing

Prospects
What type(s) of performing can I do?

What individuals or companies do I know that already utilize performers in my area of expertise?

What businesses do I patronize that need performers?

Allies
Which individuals and groups have capacity to support my goal to perform?

Information
What do I already know about performing and what do I want/need to learn about performing?

What resources (books, articles, websites, specialists/experts, etc.) can support my efforts to improve my performance skills?

Dollars
How much money can I make performing?

What next step will I make to begin getting P-A-I-D to perform?

CONCLUSION

Although there are many other ways to supplement your teaching income, I decided to stop at ten because, in the beloved words of the late, great Mary Kay Ash, "A confused mind does nothing."

Over the years, I've tried to share business ideas with colleagues and show them how *they* could personally supplement or even replace their full-time teaching income, but like my peers in Mrs. Burson's education literacy class at ASU, they appeared agitated, as if they thought I was just bragging. So, as one of my best friends told me in an email she wrote in 2005, when I was considering marrying my then boyfriend and uprooting my sons to move with him from Georgia to Texas, "I decided to write to you instead of having another conversation, because you can't respond or argue with me. Writing makes the conversation one-sided and I need you to HEAR me." Like my friend, I need you to hear me. There are many ways for you to become a P-A-I-D educator. Try one and build from there. Whether you're a math teacher or not, you know nothing plus nothing AND nothing from nothing leaves nothing! You've gotta start with SOMETHING if you want to get PAID! The purpose of *The PAID Educator* is to light your pilot. Which of these professional salary supplements might you want to try?

10 PROFESSIONAL WAYS TO SUPPLEMENT YOUR TEACHING SALARY

1. **Editing:** Get P-A-I-D for preparing written material for publication by correcting, condensing, or modifying it.
2. **Proofreading:** Get P-A-I-D for reading proofs or written/printed materials and marking errors.
3. **Researching:** Get P-A-I-D for investigation.
4. **Grants:** Get P-A-I-D for writing proposals for funding.
5. **Web Content:** Get P-A-I-D for writing relevant information for websites.
6. **Articles:** Get P-A-I-D for writing information for a collection of publications.

7. **Presenting:** Get P-A-I-D for sharing information at conferences or during professional development.
8. **Consulting:** Get P-A-I-D for providing contractual services, such as site visits and on-site assessment and evaluation.
9. **Products:** Get P-A-I-D for selling materials you create or use frequently.
10. **Performances:** Get P-A-I-D for providing entertainment or visual arts.

Here are a few important tips to support your efforts to get P-A-I-D.

Operate with Integrity

Integrity is the quality of being honest and having strong moral principles. Along the way, I've intentionally brought colleagues along with me. The only issue has been the varying moral practices. The reason my career has soared is due to the way I operate—not just business, but relationships, too. When I am contracted for an opportunity, I fulfill the deliverables in those contracts with high standards and quality. Whether I'm providing products or services, I seek to do it right or not at all. Some daily tasks have been difficult to manage, especially prior to the advancement of technology. My ideas preceded the availability of software with functionality to do what I wanted at a particular time. Now, new software programs have enabled expansion and smoothed operations while providing greater benefits. In my effort to keep products affordable for clients and fellow educators, I admit to being too hands-on when I should hire someone else to complete certain tasks. Nevertheless, my intentions are always pure and I want to yield the best results possible. It is often said, "Good help is hard to find." I don't want to believe that, because I see "good people" working and doing good deeds everyday. If people strive to be more considerate and honest, the world would be a better place. All we can do is start with ourselves.

Listen to Your Elders
I've been blessed to have educators in my life who didn't mind sharing their experiences working in and out of the classroom at different levels. Better yet, I'm blessed to have crossed paths with educators who consistently work outside the classroom—some while working a full-time position and others who are successful working independently. I've also been influenced by educators who've shared failures and

missed opportunities. I learned to only take advice from those who had worked for themselves at some point, because they could provide realistic information and not just anecdotes.

Trudy Friar, the lead trainer of my TFT course at Gainesville College back in 2001, became a close friend and colleague throughout the years. Early on in my consulting career, actually right after I completed the TFT course, she advised it would take about five years to build my reputation to a point where people would know me by name, and my contracts should increase to a level where I could quit my full-time job teaching at the university and work independently, if I wanted. She warned me not to quit my job prematurely. I'm so happy she offered me such sound advice and that I listened. For, it was 2006, five and a half years after starting my consulting and training company, that I resigned from my full-time job. By then, I was Director of Instruction of the Division of Early Care and Education and Academic Programs at Albany Technical College. I was starting to feel settled and content in the position, which I'd accepted in 2002, when tragedy struck reminding me of my original goal to become my own boss. One of my faculty members, Bernice, who had always warned me about working so much and spending time with my sons, died in a car accident one evening after work. She was my most supportive subordinate and mother of an only child who had just gone off to college. I could hear Bernice's voice saying, "Alright now. You'd better get some rest. When you're dead and gone, they're gonna find someone to replace you and forget you were even here." Well, Bernice passed away after 5 PM one evening, and I had all eight of her classes covered before 11 AM the next morning, after receiving repeated calls and emails from the instructional team asking who's going to teach all her classes. Bernice was speaking to me from the grave. Just like she used to tell me, we had replaced her and moved on like she never existed. It was just business as usual for my colleagues, but I was in mourning. I miss her dearly. She made me a better mother and a more balanced professional. After she died, I submitted my resignation less than two weeks later, and began working for myself, which enabled me to spend more time with my sons.

Bravely Face Obstacles
In 2001, when Dr. Perkins and I were approved to present our SIP and YTA grant programs at a conference in Toronto, Canada, not only was it my

very first time traveling by air, but I was six months pregnant with my second son. On several occasions, I wanted to tell Dr. Perkins I didn't want to travel at this stage in my pregnancy, but being an unwed mother, I wanted to prove I was just as efficient as any other faculty member on campus, if not more. Buzz was already spreading around campus causing me to feel my job was in jeopardy, so I wanted to demonstrate my value. If I had not gone on this trip, I would've never met the professor from Georgia College and State University who created the literacy curriculum, which inspired me to write WINGS Curriculum. Nor would I have met the faculty member from San Francisco who had taken a year sabbatical to work on a toy project as a consultant with Mattel. I didn't even know what a sabbatical was when I met her, let alone that I could leave my job to conduct research or work on a project and return at a later date. Over a decade later, when Bright Starts/Kids II invited me to work as a consultant writing web content for their toys and gear for babies and young children, she was the first person who came to mind. The entire trip was a pleasure and there were no hiccups. I'm so happy I didn't give in to my fears. My doctor cleared me to go, so I went, big and pregnant, and was filled with inspiration for future projects and products.

I experienced yet another dilemma in the summer of 2001, after my son was born. When I first saw the TFT brochure requiring five days of training at Gainesville College, which was four hours north of where I lived at the time, I almost didn't take it. I didn't realize the significance of the course and all I could do by completing it. That is, until I took the brochure to my Department Chair at the university and she denied my professional leave request. Her actual response was, "Naw, you could offer classes and make money doing your own thang." I was advised by another colleague that she could offer the same course at the university, so I wouldn't have to take off from work. I'm so thankful I didn't listen to either of them. I decided to take personal days and focus on my personal and business goals. My son's father and I drove four hours from Albany, Georgia up to Gainesville, Georgia with both our five-month old son and my four year-old son. I booked a room at a hotel right across the street from the college, so I would be close enough to go over and breastfeed our baby during breaks. Completing the TFT at Gainesville College enabled me to build my training business to new heights and depths. From that point on, I have continued to manage and build it as a consulting company, while intermittently teaching at the university level—sometimes full-time, but primarily as an adjunct instructor. It turns out that ASU could not offer the course, as my colleague promised. For, this was a unique program that was fairly new and solely approved by the state. It was so new that my trainer approval code is six. I shudder to think what might have happened had I not taken the course when I did.

Become Technically Proficient

The year was 2000. I was sitting in Dean of Education Claude Perkins' office at Albany State University for my first annual faculty performance review. One of the requirements he set for the College of Education was for all faculty to complete InTECH Training—a full course on integrating technology, primarily the Microsoft Office Suite, into teacher education. Facilitated by the college's on-site Educational Technology Training Center, the course was FREE. And guess what? I didn't take it! Dean Perkins showed me no mercy. He calmly asked why I didn't complete or even register for the course. My honest, but ridiculous, response was, "Well, nobody else took it either." Oooooh! If you could have seen the look on his face. He gave me a lecture on initiative, independence, and self-directedness that would facilitate my success and change my life. This experience taught me the importance of maximizing my full potential.

Once I completed InTECH Training, I learned to develop online components for all my college courses, integrate technology into teaching young children, develop impressive presentations, and manipulate prevalent education/business software. Now, whether I am devising or conducting training, developing or teaching college courses, exploring new software, designing online components for my companies and personal brand, employing interactive social media strategies, or engaging in research, all it takes is a few clicks for me to gain familiarity and begin operation with any new software I encounter. Everything I do as a professional and entrepreneur is highly infused with technology, which I have the ability to develop myself. However, I meet so many supposed professionals who only know how to access and navigate social media sites. They need a Dr. Perkins in their lives to light a fire up-under them. Dr. Claude G. Perkins is now President of Virginia Union University and one of my favorite mentors of all-time. He was hard on me, but for good reason. As a young, blooming professional, he knew I had gifts inside me that simply needed nurturing. Thank you, Dr. Perkins!

I admonish you to acquire some new technological skills by taking advantage of local resources, colleges and universities, continuing education programs, on-the-job training opportunities, and/or community programs. The school or institution where you work likely offers free technology training opportunities for faculty and staff. Technology is a lasting part of our ever-evolving future. Wouldn't you rather have it as your friend, rather than foe? Find out what professional development is available at little or no cost to you and start registering NOW.

Get Comfortable Tooting Your Own Horn
In 2009, my childhood neighbor and friend, Lethia Owens, who is now a world-renowned speaker and entrepreneur, advised me to create an account on all the major social media platforms—Facebook, Twitter, and LinkedIn, at the time. Building a business and reputation in today's society requires social media exposure and connections. If you work in a silo, no one will know who you are, what you do, and how well you do it. It's important to post at least once per day, even if it's just a picture and/or quote about your industry

or work. Your goal is to establish yourself as an expert or specialist in your industry.

You should also consider securing a small, inexpensive website to house all your products, samples, and photos of your work in one public place. Whenever you tweet, post, or pin, be sure to use the hashtag symbol (#) as a means to categorize your information, which enables users to easily locate topics of interest and facilitate the trending of topics. Your posts should frequently lead users to your website. Social networking sites have incorporated the hashtag as a way to identify and search for key words or topics. Simply stated, the hashtag allows us to tag data—similar to how we tag pictures. Hashtags enable social media to make the world smaller. Connections I've made with varied associates afford me countless opportunities in business, television, radio, news, magazines and other publications, largely because I intentionally hashtag key words or phrases when posting to social media. If you're an expert on a topic, you should let the world know it by tagging any information (data) you post. Every profession needs to be able to identify its experts. From this point forward, just before sharing a tweet, post, or pin, ask yourself, *which words or phrases in this post are significant in my expertise, work, hobbies, or interests.* Then, add no more than three hashtags to your tweet or post. Remember to engage with other users in your industry by clicking on the hashtags and liking, reposting, retweeting, or pinning any of their posts you like. Be sure to check out related tweets and posts, especially on Facebook, Twitter, LinkedIn and Instagram. You just might learn something new or make a life-changing connection! This is a task you MUST make time for or hire someone competent enough to do it for you. Use social media management software like TweetDeck Buffer, or HootSuite to schedule your posts to multiple social media sites. And don't forget to join relevant groups on Facebook and LinkedIn. This is where you will find information to complete your P-A-I-D strategies, especially when trying to determine the *dollars* you can make for different positions. I guarantee there have already been conversations related to pay. You just need to view the archived discussions in the groups you join.

Consort with Like-minded People
Any time we have a new idea or goal, it is natural to want to share it with individuals who are closest to us. I must advise against that when considering starting a new venture, especially if it's out of the norm or if you

have a desire to expand it to become fully independent one day. The average person will start quoting clichés and deter you, especially if they've never started a business of their own or worked outside of a traditional job. I recommend you find your tribe, folks who are thinking just like you and those who have followed through on their goals and dreams.

At one time, no one in my circle seemed to understand why I would quit a "good-paying job with benefits" to work for myself. So, I had to get myself some new associates. I went on Meetup.com to find groups related to my needs and interests. I joined a couple of author groups that met once or twice per month and allowed each author to read a chapter from the books we were writing, followed by individual detailed feedback. I also found a group of women who met for a monthly business luncheon, during which attendees were allowed to introduce themselves and share information about their businesses.

One of my favorites was an entrepreneurial group who met monthly in the back of an art gallery to discuss their businesses. Everyone was allowed to stand in front of the group and give their elevator pitch, and time was allotted for participants to network with individuals they felt the need to connect. It was at this event where

I met new and budding authors, as well as like-minded individuals who all just wanted to be their own bosses and call their own shots on their own terms. Everyone in this group told the dirty truth about the ebbs and flows in business and unlimited hours required to build, grow and expand. I also learned from this group that it's okay to work full-time until your business can consistently replace your income and benefits. Better yet, if ebbs last too long or a recession hits, it's perfectly okay to accept a full-time or part-time position, until you can get your business back up to the standard needed to replace your income. That's what we went to college for in the first place. A good thing about being an educator is that children and schools are everywhere, so we can intermittently reactivate our teaching careers and be welcomed back with open arms.

Building Lasting Relationships

There is no way I could have achieved so many goals and successes without building relationships with people, who eventually became my *allies*. Whenever you meet people, it's important to treat them with respect and remember that no one is perfect and everyone is NOT prejudice, jealous, or against you. People who don't look like me have been some of my greatest allies. For example, Dr. Anita Smith and I are still connected and meet for lunch periodically to check in. She continues to serve as my professional reference and mentors me on career opportunities, retirement, and other topics. I adore her career trajectory, personable spirit, and commitment to civil rights—breaking through barriers for decades to ensure EVERYONE had access to high-quality professional development and career advancement.

Living in the deep south, I grew up listening to stories about race and advice on how to make choices given my environment. As I've traveled and cultivated my career, I eventually realized the *average* person simply likes being in the company of good people, regardless of the color of their skin. When I wrote WINGS Curriculum, I went back and forth with my publisher, Frank, about whether or not I should include my photo on the back of the curriculum manual. As a white man who I can only assume did not grow up experiencing racial tension, he looked at me with a perplexed expression. After a brief pause, he responded, "Bisa, you are a highly educated, intelligent and experienced professional. In my experience, that's all people really care about. Customers will make a purchase when they trust the product and the person who created it." Thank you for helping me get out of my own head and get WINGS off the ground, Frank Harris. You treated WINGS as if it was your own baby.

I've maintained a lasting relationship with my former colleagues and administrators in the school systems and colleges where I've worked. I conduct training for the school system where I taught first grade back in the 90's. They even adopted and implemented WINGS Curriculum in their Pre-K program, so do the early learning programs at ASU and Albany Tech. I still visit the high school where I recently taught for three years to support my former students' new ECE instructor in implementing the CDA program—and at no charge to the school because I want to ensure the program continues to progress and not suffer due to my decision to leave. Of course, I miss my students and love to engage with them. I was able to see an entire cohort of students complete the ECE pathway, while I was employed there. The students who were my *babies* in my ECE I course became independent and could practically run the program on their own by my third year, when they were in ECE III. They could manage the children enrolled in our early morning program effectively and even trained the ECE II students who were coming up behind them. I am so happy I accepted the position at the high school. The only puzzle I have yet to complete is how to help my colleagues who have the desire to do what I've done. They wonder how I'm out here *surviving in these streets* without that $4,000+ paycheck I had to wait to receive at the end of each month. If only they knew. It's my hope that *The P-A-I-D Educator* lifts fellow educators' blindfolds and affords them the income they truly desire.

As long as you are intentional about building diverse relationships throughout your career, multiple opportunities will result, enabling you to support others and others to support you. For those of you who grew up experiencing any sort of stereotype, you must remind yourself that God only created one YOU. None of us are exactly like anyone else and that is what makes the world so beautiful. Discover your purpose and take your rightful place in society. Let's strive to leave our mark on the world. Whatever your mark may be, you can make a difference during your "dash"—the short time we are here on this earth from birth to death. Just know that we are better when we work together.

Celebrate Your Milestones
When I introduced WINGS Curriculum in 2009, one of my colleagues asked me, "Bisa, do you ever celebrate

yourself?" I was like, "Huh?" She urged me to start celebrating my accomplishments, even the small ones, with some type of festivity—a meal or a drink with close friends, an event, a trip...something! I must admit, that was great advice. However, I am still learning to follow-through with self-celebrations. I am usually moving on to the next venture and forget to even acknowledge my successes. That has to stop! One thing I have learned over the years is people are generally so busy in their own worlds that the last thing on their minds is celebrating someone else. So, what must we do? That's right, celebrate ourselves. If we don't toot our own horns, who will? Bravo, self! I must be honest. I am still learning to celebrate myself. Believe it or not, I am fairly modest about my accomplishments and always strive to do more. Even when I am speaking or presenting workshops, I hate to introduce myself and only started when participants would pull me aside during small-group activities or breaks to ask, usually with excitement, what I do and what have I done in my career. I realized I was doing them a disservice, because people who attend speakers' sessions are really interested in the person, not just the content presented. You must remember *it's who you know AND who knows you*. We are all only one connection away from our destiny, which will often occur through one key individual. We never know who that individual might be, so treat everyone with respect and kindness – online and offline.

"TEACHERS MAKE *ALL* OTHER PROFESSIONS POSSIBLE!"

So, give yourself some credit for all the success you've inspired and enabled amongst your former students. It would be nice if teachers could receive stipends, honorariums, or royalties for all the seeds we've planted that have sprouted and yielded a vast harvest. But, given that is unlikely to happen, it's okay to experience further success of your own. Give yourself permission to grow, shine, and earn. Despite what people say, money is NOT the root of all evil; it's "the love of money." God wants His children to live our best lives during the short time we are here on this earth. Earning extra money is necessary. Stop making excuses and start making plans to get PAID!

And, as you learn, don't forget to pay it forward with our fellow colleagues. Let's continue to bring others along for the ride.

SPECIAL ACKNOWLEDGMENTS

The P-A-I-D Educator would not be possible without the care and guidance from all the educators in my life who noticed and nurtured my individual differences and quirks. It took many years for me to learn just how important and beneficial my personal characteristics would become in the trajectory of my career. I want the world to know how much I appreciate my favorite teachers from preschool through college: My preschool teacher/director Ms. Daniels; fourth grade teacher Ms. Denise Carter; fifth grade teacher Mrs. Patricia Gilbert-Parker; sixth grade English teacher Ms. Darol McGhee; seventh grade English teachers, Mrs. Minnie Suttles and Patricia Alford; high school Literature teachers Mrs. Anita Tunstall and Dr. Valerie Overstreet-

Thomas; college professors Mrs. Denise Burson-Beckwith, Dr. Deborah Bembry, and Dr. Babatunde Abayomi.

Thank you, Mama and Pop, for showing me the importance of working outside the box! Thank you to my brother, Corey, for calling to check on me and uplifting me regularly. My sister, "Glee," for telling me early-on to remember that I am the prize. My late Uncle Rob for being my daddy when my father, his brother, was on the road.

And, most of all, to my sons, Cameron and Jordan, thank you for making motherhood so wonderful and such a pleasure. Being your mom has been a blessing, the title I value most, and the greatest accomplishment of my life! I love you both!

Last, but never least, Father God, thank You for showing me favor, for whatever reason. Thank You for saving me at a young age and for never leaving or forsaking me, despite my actions. I am nothing without You and everything because of You! You light up my life!

ABOUT THE AUTHOR

Dr. Bisa Batten Lewis, affectionately known as "Dr. Bisa," is Founder and CEO of Ideal Early Learning, LLC and WINGS Curriculum, LLC, and President & CEO of the Dr. Bisa Foundation. She is a published author of education and parenting articles, college textbooks, children's books and music, and *WINGS: The Ideal Curriculum for Children in Preschool*—a nationally recognized learning system for children from infancy to age five. Working as an educator and administrator for over 25 years, from lab schools to the university level, Dr. Bisa is a diversely experienced education authority and renowned public speaker.

Dr. Bisa earned her Doctor of Education and Master of Education degrees in Adult Education at the University of Georgia and Master of Education and Bachelor of Science degrees in Early Childhood

Education at Albany State University. She was elected as President of Black Child Development Institute (BCDI)—Atlanta in May 2018, where she has administered the establishment of significant partnerships, programs and initiatives to improve the quality of life for children and families.

Professing as a life goal to advocate for children, she is actively committed to upgrading the quality of education settings around the world. Dr. Bisa's mantra is: "Die empty; the cemetery has no use for your potential."

CPSIA information can be obtained
at www.ICGtesting.com
Printed in the USA
BVHW040959210120
570065BV00009B/35